To Bill and

Shaping up:
Re-forming Reformed Worship

Best wishes

Ernest
October 2005

Ernest Marvin

Foreword by B. A. Gerrish

The
United
Reformed
Church

ISBN 0 85346 238 0

© Ernest Marvin, 2005

Published by The United Reformed Church

86 Tavistock Place, London WC1H 9RT

The source of each extract quoted is given in the appropriate footnote.

*Scripture passages are from the New Revised Standard Version of the Bible, copyright
1989 by the Division of Christian Education of the National Council of the Churches
of Christ in the USA. Used by permission. All rights reserved.*

*The publisher is grateful to all who have granted permisssion for their work to be used.
Any corrections or additions should be addressed to the Secretary, Communications
and Editorial Committee, The United Reformed Church, 86 Tavistock Place, London
WC1H 9RT, and will be amended in any future addition.*

Produced by Communications and Editorial, Graphics Office

Printed by Compass Press Ltd, 162-164 Upper Richmond Road, 2nd Floor, London SW15 2SL

Acknowledgements

This book has occupied quite a deal of my post-retirement liberty but it only began to 'shape up' over the past twelve months. That it did so owed a great deal to the advice and encouragement of several friends and acquaintances. None of them can be held accountable for the views herein expressed, but I wish to record my indebtedness for their help, advice and occasional admonishments.

Pride of place must go to the Reverend David Gardner of Leicester, good friend and fellow minister in the United Reformed Church in the United Kingdom. David must feel that he has lived with this book almost as intimately as I have. He has visited me on innumerable occasions and we have spent many hours in mutual discussion and gentle argument. At several stages I have taken on board his suggestions, as well as more felicitous ways of expressing my ideas and points of view. Throughout the whole enterprise he has been a source of great encouragement, especially at those times when I did begin to wonder if, perhaps, I should quietly put the project to one side. I hope that he is able to detect the improvements that followed on his many comments.

I also owe a debt to another good friend, the Reverend Professor Horace T. Allen, Jr., Emeritus Professor of Worship and Preaching at Boston University School of Theology. He has been an inspirational teacher of worship and preaching to many students for the ministry down the years, and a powerful representative of the Reformed position in the course of major ecumenical debates concerning liturgy and the lectionary. In what follows there is probably much more than I realise which is a direct result of my 'sitting at his feet' over a considerable period of time.

I am most grateful to those who have read the manuscript in full and yet encouraged me to seek publication! Their support does not mean that they have agreed with everything I have written. In this regard my thanks are due to the late Professor Shirley Guthrie, Professor George Stroup, Dr Andrew Fullerton, the Reverend Keith Riglin, Professor Roy Niblett and, of course, Professor Brian Gerrish who wrote the Foreword. I am particularly grateful to the latter for doing so at a time when he was both very much involved with the final stages of publications of his own but also facing major surgery.

Others have generously given me advice on specific points, and I thank Dr David Thompson for saving me from an over simplification in one important respect.

The laborious task of preparing the index and proof-reading the typescript was cheerfully and efficiently undertaken by Nicholas Morgan.

My neighbour, Gerhard Hattingh, generously placed his computing skills at my disposal deciphering my wayward typing 'skills'.

Above all I would like to thank Carol Rogers, the Secretary for Communications, and Sara Foyle, The URC Graphic Artist, for their encouragement and professionalism throughout. I could not have had a more careful and helpful editor and designer.

A final acknowledgement must be given to those to whom this book is dedicated – the Congregations of St Andrew's, Sheffield, and St Columba's, Cambridge. I was minister at the former for nearly ten years and at the latter for fourteen. I was fortunate in the extreme to be called to two churches whose worship already demonstrated much which is advocated in the following pages, but who were not averse to change if they saw good reason for it.

Ernest Marvin

Cheltenham, June 2005.

Foreword

'Worship Wars' is the now familiar slogan that came into vogue in the British and American churches during the second half of the last century, and the dispute is still with us. The adversaries line up as champions of either 'traditional' or 'contemporary' worship. Those who stand for contemporary worship are rebelling against what they take to be the moribund style of older church services. For this reason, it might be more precise to speak of a revolt – a revolutionary war. And two things need to be said at the outset: there were good reasons to raise the banner of protest against the old style of worship, and there are good reasons to think that something of value may be lost in the new.

Nobody denies there were provocations that justified the protest; declining attendance at Sunday services, especially in Britain, made the problem obvious. I should speak only of the so-called English Free Churches with which, as a young man, I was most familiar: the Presbyterians and the Congregationalists, now joined in the United Reformed Church. The malaise was not confined to them, and some of their churches were less affected by it than others. But, in general, the besetting sin of Reformed worship was a heavy didacticism, the minister addressing the congregation as though it were a class of keen (or sullen) schoolchildren. The sermon so dominated that sometimes it was only by a judgment of charity that one could speak of an order of worship at all–and not just a 'hymn sandwich'. On those rare Sundays when Holy Communion was celebrated, a misplaced benediction encouraged many worshippers to run for the exit before the bread and wine were uncovered. The mood was grave, all the more so when the opening prayer was reduced to a confession of sins. And the penitential tone was carried over into the sacrament: Calvary was remembered, but not from *this* side of the Saviour's resurrection. It was particularly the young who objected that church was dull and stiff, lacking in a lively sense of community. If they stayed, they wanted a more animated, less formal pattern of worship, relevant to contemporary tastes and style. They had a point, and still have. So does the traditionalist, who criticises their critique.

But on what basis is the argument pursued? What are the tests of sound worship? Innovations are often proposed and resisted as though it were all a matter of what we *like*. Maybe it is inevitable in our consumer culture that the church's leaders should wish to find out what the customer wants, and to provide it; otherwise, the pews will be empty. But they also have the responsibility to keep before us the fundamental question, 'What, after all, *is* worship?' and to remind us that for some two thousand years before us Christians have thought about the pattern (or patterns) of worship suited to the revelation of God in Jesus Christ. If the advocates of contemporary changes do not always begin, as they should, by asking about the meaning of Christian worship, the traditionalist response to them is sometimes not traditional enough–resting, perhaps, on reluctance to change what we've been doing for ten or twelve years.

The author of this admirable book defines worship as 'a response to a persistent claim upon our lives'. No one would agree more completely than John Calvin, who found the heart of the entire Christian life in Paul's words, 'Do you not know . . . that you are not your own? For you were bought with a price' (I Corinthians 6.19-20). And Christian worship is nothing if it does not represent and enact our Christian life as belonging to God. This is by no means to say that 'God first' sets aside human needs; rather, it identifies the deepest need of all. Calvin's catechism follows up its affirmation that the chief *end* of human life is to know God, who placed us in this world to be glorified in us, with the question, 'What is the highest *good* of humans?' Answer: 'The very same thing.' Martin Luther, to whom Calvin owed so much, would also agree that worship is 'a response to a persistent claim upon our lives'. He found the *meaning* of Christian worship in the story of Jesus and the ten lepers (Luke 17.11-19). Ten were healed, but only one turned back and fell at Jesus' feet in gratitude. 'This is true worship', Luther comments, 'to turn back and with a loud voice glorify God. . . . Oh, how few they are who so turn back–scarce one in ten.'

On the *shape* of Christian worship there has been an energetic renewal of liturgical study that crosses denominational lines–and a striking measure of convergence, if not a full consensus. The findings have been incorporated into new service manuals such as the 1993 *Book of Common Worship* of the Presbyterian

Church (U.S.A.), the church to which I now belong. In the absence of an old-fashioned act of uniformity, there is no guarantee that the new service books will everywhere be used and studied; and most of us accept the 'pluralist' view that flexibility and variety are compatible with agreement on theological and liturgical principles. On one such principle there is, I believe, near unanimity: that the norm of Christian worship is a service of Word *and* Sacrament. Calvin's desire for weekly Communion ('at least once a week') may be closer to fulfilment in the Reformed churches than ever before. There is also general recognition that the *anamnesis* ('remembrance') of I Corinthians 11.24-25 is more than a mental recollection of events in the past. Here, too, Calvin is vindicated. When Bullinger insisted to him that the Lord's Supper is remembrance, Calvin replied, 'I say that in the Lord's Supper there is remembrance of a *present* reality'.

All of these themes—and many more—are opened up in the pages of Ernest Marvin's book.

Besides his account of the current situation in the churches and the meaning and shape of Christian worship, he shares his thoughts on hymns, the sermon, prayer, the lectionary, the children's talk, the creed, the sacraments, the offering, and on things that may be unfamiliar to some readers: the Little Entrance, the Great Entrance, the Peace, and the Epiclesis. My mind goes back to the years we shared at Westminster College, Cambridge, the 'seminary' of the then Presbyterian Church of England. As a keen evangelical, I was instinctively suspicious of talk about 'the church' and 'the liturgy'. Though baptized in the Church of England, it had been my good fortune to become a member of Westminster Chapel, where the extraordinary sermons of D. Martyn Lloyd-Jones (the 'Doctor', as everyone called him) did not leave the congregation with any sense that something might be liturgically lacking. It was from Ernest and another friend at Westminster College that I learned about the liturgical interests of the Iona Community, and this—along with my reading of William D. Maxwell's writings—opened up a whole new world to me. In 1955 we went our separate ways, but we have remained, for the most part, of one mind about the meaning and shape of worship.

Ernest Marvin's *Shaping up: Re-forming Reformed Worship* is a worthy successor to Maxwell's *Concerning Worship*. Maxwell held that a good churchman will not confuse the importance of the sermon with the popularity of the preacher or the singularity of his gifts, but will teach his people that they come to pay honour to God: 'He will direct their thoughts towards the majesty and glory of God, and quicken their sense of duty towards Him.' Ernest believes that an 'unmistakable emphasis on God's transcendence and holiness' marked the traditional act of worship, and that it is the particular responsibility of the Reformed churches to recapture and reaffirm this emphasis along with the recovery of 'liturgical shape'. He writes, like Maxwell, out of a rich pastoral experience as well as assiduous thought and study. But his style is quite different: informal, colloquial, enlivened by wonderful stories–dare one say, thoroughly 'contemporary'? He balances theological insight with practical wisdom, passionate conviction with an affirmation of openness and flexibility, and doesn't hesitate to draw attention to 'irritants' as well as to serious deviations of principle from sound liturgical norms. He may not convince every reader on all counts, but his book will help move the Worship Wars to serious, mutually respectful, and informed conversation.

The Revd Professor B. A. Gerrish
John Nuveen Professor Emeritus
The University of Chicago Divinity School

CONTENTS

**To the elders and congregations of
St Columba's Cambridge and St Andrew's Sheffield.**

Introduction

Reformed or Deformed?

David only came occasionally to church. He was seventeen and had a different agenda from that of his parents, albeit one he shared with the majority of his peers. It was obvious that, when he did come, it was only out of affection and respect for the former, which was no bad thing.

'David!', I ventured to say one Sunday morning during coffee hour, 'I notice you never sing the hymns; why not?' 'I only sing when I'm happy and I'm never happy in church'. There was no quick answer to that, but what should worship have done for David?

Worship is a response, a response to a persistent claim upon our lives, but if no claim is felt then no response is possible. Of course the experience of a strong claim upon one's life is not the sole preserve of the religiously inclined. It may have its source in another human being – 'I worship the ground she walks upon' – or it may originate from witnessing a beautiful sunset or hearing a stunning piece of music – 'It took me out of myself' – or whatever. But the particular activity in which Christians, Jews, Muslims, Hindus and others engage, and speak of as worship, certainly differs in kind, if not always in degree, from this 'worship' at the human level. Most religions assert that their worship is a response to the divine, to that which is beyond. It was this experience which David seemingly did not have, so therefore he could not respond to it with praise. (It was interesting, nonetheless, that he associated the state of being happy as a prerequisite for the act of worship. This is a mistake that is also commonly made by many Christians, hence those fixed smiles that can drive the rest of us crazy. But this is not our concern at the moment – see chapter 7 'Celebration').

Why do Christians worship God? We do so because of our belief that this God created us to worship him. As the Westminster Confession's first article put it: 'Man's (*sic*) chief and highest end is to glorify God, and fully to enjoy him for ever.' (The Westminster Confession was the profession of Presbyterian faith as set out by the Westminster Assembly, 1643-1653.) We believe that God created us in his image, and one that would reflect his glory. But Christians also believe that not only did he create us to worship him, but also that he commanded us to do so. The first four of the Ten Commandments concern worship. (Exodus 20:1-7.)

Commandments, however, which came into existence in ancient times are all very well, but most of us need something more corporeal to which we can respond. Christians believe that this has been provided by the Christ event, Jesus 'who became man' (the Nicene Creed), God's free gift to us. The new Christians of the first century CE made the exciting discovery of the sheer gratuitousness of God's act in sending Jesus to them (there was no need for God so to act), and it overwhelmed them (eg Ephesians 1:3-6) They recognised, as had their Jewish forebears, the absolute *worth* of God. He alone was worthy of their devotion and their 'worth' ship.

'Whom have I in heaven but you? And there is nothing on earth that I desire other than you'. (Psalm 73:25.) The only response possible was one of praise and thanksgiving, namely worship.

When worship is mentioned in the following pages it will denote that activity in which Christians engage, mainly, but not always, in church on a Sunday, to honour God. The Scriptures, however, of both the Old and New Testaments stress that honouring God does not consist simply of the words we offer up in the sanctuary. There is also an important place for the offering of service in the world for the furthering of God's glory and purposes. It should become apparent later on that this has been taken into account, but the main concern of this book is that aspect of worship that takes place when Christians gather together to praise God, to wait on his Word, and to celebrate the sacraments.

This intention arises out of the recognition that what happens in church on a Sunday means less and less to many in our Western Society than it used to do. This is not to suggest that all those who never darken the door of a church are unbelievers. Some do have more than a residual belief in God, perhaps even accompanied by a prayer life that could shame many a Christian, but they feel no need for a corporate expression of their faith.

This book is mainly concerned with present day worship in what are known as the Reformed churches, but it also seeks to address the subject as it affects the whole Church of God at this time. But, as the title indicates, the state of play in churches of the Reformed tradition is our main interest.

So which are the Reformed churches?

Today the term 'Reformed' requires explaining in a way that would have been unnecessary a few years ago. In recent visits to the USA I have asked many people whose churches are historically in this tradition what it meant to them. In the majority of cases they had either not heard of the term or did not consider it was of any special relevance. Sad to say, such increasingly seems to be the case with a similar constituency in the UK today.

Without outlining a potted history, which would only delay matters somewhat, it is sufficient for our purposes simply to say that the word 'Reformed' describes those denominations that arose in the sixteenth century as a protest against the belief system, structures and morality of the church of that day. In Britain in the aftermath of the great schism of English Protestantism of 1662, it broke into several forms which are still recognisable. These include some Anglicans/Episcopalians (but not all), the Church of Scotland (and other Presbyterians), Congregationalists and Baptists. Methodists came later but some Methodists are sympathetic towards this tradition and are more comfortable with it than with any other, apart from their own.

I am a minister of the United Reformed Church, a church which came into being in 1972 as the result of the union between the Presbyterian Church of England and the Congregational Church in England and Wales. This first alignment between members of the Reformed family in the UK since the Reformation welcomed the Re-formed Association of Churches of Christ of Great Britain and Ireland (known in the USA as the Disciples of Christ) into its fellowship in 1981 and most of the Congregational churches in Scotland in April 2000.

The bulk of the illustrative material in these pages comes out of ministries in Bristol, Sheffield, Cambridge and the United States; but in recent years extensive visits to Canada, South Korea, Japan, South Africa, France and Hungary have also contributed to my perceptions. Although what follows is written from a British perspective, the contents and reading list will indicate how much I owe especially to my acquaintance with a number of churches and denominations in the United States.

The United Reformed Church is a member of the World Alliance of Reformed Churches, the combined membership of which is quite considerable. The significance of this is not always recognised within Anglican and Roman Catholic circles, nor to any great extent within their mutual dialogues, and this raises interesting questions which go beyond the scope of this book.

The Church from which I retired as a working minister in 1996 had changed a great deal from the one into whose ministry I was ordained in 1955 – much more than it had changed in any of the previous years of the twentieth century. There have been changes for the better, but there are also others which have not been so. It is the latter which are mainly addressed in these pages but not, (I hope), in a spirit of pessimism or pique. They are, however, given prominence out of concern for many people who feel they have been almost 'unchurched' by recent trends.

I also write out of a concern that, as well as regular attenders, the modern seeker after a faith is being 'short-changed' by what is on offer in many of our sanctuaries. 'De-formed' rather than 'Reformed' would be a more accurate description, albeit a harsh one, of what sometimes is available.

The worship and the ministry of Word and Sacraments in today's church are the main preoccupations in all that follows, closely aligned to the conviction that we have much still to learn on these two matters from the teaching of John Calvin (1509-1564), one of the 'greats' among the Reformers of the sixteenth century. His influence is not confined to this one section of the Church catholic, and I hope that what is said here about him will strike a sympathetic chord with those who are not within the Reformed tradition as such, and help to portray another side to the great reformer that is often obscured.

I also hope that it will soon become clear that I am not involved in an attempt to defend traditional ways at all costs and against all comers, and at the expense of the true needs of the modern world. There have been, in the past twenty years or so, enough hatchet jobs done on the present state of the church, but it still survives. I make no apology for lapsing, from time to time, into an autobiographical mode, utilising personal stories from the church of my youth right up until the present day which, I hope, will underline my love for, and debt to, the Church in which I was baptised.

But what is the nature of Reformed worship? Essentially, it reflects the basis of Reformed teaching (theology) which stresses the sovereignty of God, the centrality of God in the life of the individual and in the life of the world: God first. We do not have a monopoly on this over against other Christians, but we have a particular obligation to affirm it boldly by what we say and do in our liturgy. That we are not doing this as well as we might is part of the contention in what follows.

But is there a precise shape to Reformed worship? This is an increasingly difficult question to answer today, because of the wide spectrum of practices within those Churches which still claim to belong to the Reformed family. Therefore I propose to begin by describing two major scenarios, one from the past and one from the present, as a starting point for what is to follow. This is to demonstrate that a significant change took place in the worship of these churches during the last half of the twentieth century, one that gradually gathered momentum after the end of the Second World War and which has made a considerable impact on the ethos of the Reformed constituency. I hope that this methodology will then enable us to proceed at a more critical level as we investigate what form or forms Reformed worship should take for today if it is to be a fitting and proper vehicle for the praise and thanksgiving of the people of God in the new millennium and, at the same time, still be the 'converting and edifying ordinance' that John Calvin claimed for it, equipping them for mission and service in today's world.

Chapter One

Shaping Up

Worship:
Adoring or Anodyne

Worship: Adoring or Anodyne

I was five years old when taken for the first time by my mother and father to morning worship in a large Glasgow church. We went there whenever we were up in the big city, usually during father's summer break from the parish in the lowlands of Scotland where he was a minister of the Kirk.

I can still remember my first impressions on seeing the large central pulpit the size of a boxing ring, behind which were splayed the organ pipes, common-place then and in many Reformed sanctuaries since. It puzzled me why such seemed to be the object of devotion by the assembled company (there was never a cross to be seen). There was no such problem, however, when it came to knowing who stood in that pulpit in front of those sacred pipes – it was God Himself!

Precisely on the stroke of 11am, the divinely appointed hour for so many worshippers in my tradition then and since, the choir entered followed by a venerable old man, (or so it seemed to the child, but research shows that he was probably no more than forty years old), soberly dressed in black cassock, black Geneva gown and preaching scarf. The only concession to colour was provided by white preaching bands around his neck and a degree hood over his shoulders. His tall figure was topped with a fine head of silver hair. Above him lay a winding staircase into the pulpit which he climbed with measured tread, disappearing and reappearing as if ascending a light-house. He was followed by the church beadle ('verger' to Anglicans) who had already taken the Bible into the pulpit. The latter waited reverently until 'God' had entered the pulpit and then closed the door (*sic*) behind him. He returned whence he had come, only reappearing when 'God' required to be released at the end of the service.

How did I, at the age of five, come to the conclusion that in that place the minister was God? That was easy. First, he was closer to heaven than the rest of us, and, what with his splendid head of hair and dignified apparel and beautiful voice, he looked and sounded as I imagined God to look and sound. But, second, this conviction was confirmed when, as soon as he entered the pulpit, the choir began to sing in hushed tones the Introit: 'God is in his temple: all within keep silence'.

Not once did I doubt it, so impressive was the aura of solemnity which infused the proceedings. There he was, 'God' in his Holy Temple, and we were assembled below him. He stayed with us right to the very end, during which time he did all the talking until, with arms outstretched, we were blessed and then sent on our way.

My parents, naturally, were amused when they learned what I had thought about the experience, and it was a family joke told down the years at my expense. But the scene as described was not an isolated one, though no doubt my reaction to it was. It was replicated throughout most of the churches within the Church of Scotland and, for that matter, throughout the world of the Reformed family of churches (see Introduction). No adult would have mistaken the minister for God, but they certainly would have viewed the act of worship as a most solemn and ordered occasion, one in which the sovereignty of the Almighty was acknowledged above all other divine attributes, and where the minister played a central part in heightening their awareness of His holiness and majesty. In some parts of England, Wales, Scotland, Northern Ireland (especially the latter), the USA and a few countries of the former British Empire, the act of worship still resembles an ordered progression familiar to my generation, with its unmistakable emphasis on God's transcendence and holiness. The organ pipes may continue to occupy pride of place,(being very expensive to move), although the pulpit is now likely to be to one side, if it has not been removed altogether! The minister may still dress soberly for the occasion, and the service follow an orderly course, beginning with the invitation: 'Let us worship God' to the ending with the pronouncing of the Benediction. But this kind of minister and 'ordered' liturgy are becoming increasingly rare.

Let us move on to another scenario. It is far more likely that today's seeker after a spiritual home, and one who does not want to travel too far afield, could be faced with something very different from the church as described above. There may be a minister up-front, though not always a male, and the matter of dress will now be up to individual choice, not to mention idiosyncrasy. S/he will often be dressed in street clothes, or something even more informal. It is not unusual to find that the Geneva gown has been replaced by a polo shirt. Instead of a solemn call to worship, incorporating words from scripture, followed by the injunction, 'Let us worship God', church notices, of varying degrees of length and of little interest to the stranger who may happen to be present, will be read, but only after a cheery 'good-morning' has taken priority over the traditional call to focus first upon God and to worship him.

When the act of worship eventually gets under way (in one Reformed church I attended in South Africa these preliminaries took over twenty minutes to complete), it may not follow any specific order as such. The opening hymn may or may not be one of adoration, the only way a former generation knew how to commence a service. Instead the selection is quite likely to emphasise our fellowship together rather than addressing the One in whose gift alone true fellowship is to be found. The first prayer could well be of a chatty, impromptu nature shading prematurely into an intercessory mode with penitential undertones. The former priority of adoration followed by confession and the Gospel word of pardon no longer finds universal recognition – that opening to a service the appropriateness of which was previously unquestioned as the only possible beginning for the act of worship, irrespective of whether it happened to be a 'good' morning or a 'bad' one for those present.

Today a congregation could well be asked: 'Shall we pray?', as if a vote would then take place. In recent visits I have heard some ministers inquire before commencing the sermon: 'May I have your permission to preach in the name of the Father, the Son, and the Holy Spirit?' In such ways do some leaders of worship strive to stress that we are all equal in ministry. But we are not equal enough, it would seem, for I have yet to witness the poser of such questions wait for an answer, perhaps subconsciously recognising that God, after all, is not best worshipped through the symbolism of majority resolutions. This egalitarian emphasis is considered by its supporters to be in accord with the Reformed doctrine of the priesthood of all believers. In this they are mistaken (see chapter 13) but at least they are in no danger of mistaking the modern minister for the deity!

Soon we are into the ubiquitous Children's Address, so beloved of the adults, much less so by the children (see chapters 15 and 16). The latter will sometimes leave for their groups even before hearing a lesson from the Bible. When the scriptures are eventually read, it is not unusual to find the Gospel omitted or placed before the Epistle. The Old Testament may not even have a place at all, and this in a church which claims to be Reformed.

The singing of hymns and choruses may well be facilitated by means of a projector and overhead screen or video monitor, all of which can dwarf the traditional symbolism of pulpit, table and font, if such have not already been obscured by flowers, microphones and the minister's notes and spectacles. And so the service 'progresses'.

The above criticisms may seem an exaggerated and harsh parody, but they arise from personal observations after attending a considerable number of 'Reformed' services in different parts of the world, not least in the United States of America, since my retirement from parish ministry. Whether the frequent irritation to which I have succumbed is well-founded or simply the result of a conservative and traditional attitude, compounded by *Anno Domini*, must be judged by what follows. Nevertheless, I know that I am not alone in considering much of our worship today to be bordering on the anodyne, simply catering for emotional needs in as painless a way as possible, but not even doing that successfully. The primary purpose of worship is not to meet the needs of the people, as though any of us responsible for worship could perceive what such needs are, but to respond to the paramount need of everyone, which is simply to worship God because God is to be worshipped.

Worship should be able to comfort and reassure, but this is not its primary purpose. God is the audience, not the congregation.

But, if much present day worship leaves much to be desired, it is only fair to recognise that there were many aspects of that older tradition which had long outlived their day, the persistence of which after the end of the Second World War did little to attract a new generation to church. At this time, life in the Church of Scotland and the Presbyterian Church of England and several sister denominations was often minister-dominated. Authority resided in the Elders Meeting with the minister at its head as primus inter pares, 'first among equals', and often more primus than pares! The place of women was subsidiary to that of men, and any suggestion that they could occupy significant leadership roles either in worship or in the decision-making courts of the church, locally or nationally, was hardly countenanced. Of course in this regard the churches were simply reflecting the wider culture around them, as they have often done in the past (see chapter 17).

As for the actual worship, it tended to be on the cerebral side and followed 'the curious heresy which maintains in effect that God can hear but cannot see. Accordingly, words are held to be essential in worship, but actions to be irrelevant and intrusive.' [1] Moreover everything was in the hands of the minister, the form and content of the service being his/her responsibility alone. Holy Communion would be celebrated every quarter at most, but sometimes only twice, or even once, a year. Solemnity could quite easily shade into sombreness, and the accentuating of the transcendence of God was often at the expense of His immanence.

Of course, it is not easy to compare the two situations. One of the greatest differences between yesterday and today is that mainstream church attendance was higher then, and accompanying this fact was the understanding that worship was public, open to all. The invitation on notice boards and from pulpits was to the public worship of Almighty God (save for certain restraints when it came to communion). This allowed for anyone to feel free to slip into a pew on a Sunday and to slip away just as easily, without the fear of a visitors' book or welcoming card being thrust under their noses, never mind a propelling arm in the direction of coffee in the hall afterwards. The casual worshippers were certainly assisted in their initial desire for anonymity by the greater numbers surrounding them where they could easily get lost in the crowd. Some parts of the USA and, most certainly, South Korea provide a similar opportunity today.

These are, on the whole, very different days for the mainstream churches (or 'mainline' as they are called in the United States), certainly in the UK, with our much smaller, and falling, numbers.

---

1   William D Maxwell: Concerning Worship. Oxford University Press, 1949, p78

The outside notice boards no longer invite the passer-by to 'public worship'; instead there are posters for family services, all-age worship, theme services, contemporary worship services (very common in the USA); there are sermon titles accompanied by a promise of a very warm welcome to one and all. But, paradoxically, all this can have the opposite effect to that intended. Such announcements are more indicative of a close community, even a closed one (particularly by the liberal use of the title 'Family'), and the stranger's suspicions in this respect are often corroborated once s/he actually steps inside.

Edward Norman puts it succinctly: 'Worship as something performed to which a believer can call in, as it were, and which he or she can find familiar and easy to recognise because he or she is not required to participate in apparently spontaneous symbolic acts of human brotherhood (*sic*) known to the regular enthusiast, is less and less available. Worship as an expression of shared community values is not intended to evoke divine mysteries, and it does not do so. Its own valuable representation of an important dimension of the Christian life is, however, unavoidably limiting because it requires a new sort of initiation – into a tightly drawn community of believers.' [2] We may question Edward Norman's description of worship as a 'performance' (though see chapter 12 'High Drama') but we cannot overlook his warning concerning the excluding attitudes, (yes – often unintentional!), vis-à-vis the world demonstrated by many Christians today, not least by some of those who preside at worship. If this tendency should increase, we should not be surprised if the present gap between the sacred and the secular grows ever wider.

---

[2]   Edward Norman: Entering the Darkness – Christianity and its Modern Substitutes; London, SPCK, 1991, p74

Chapter Two

The Whole Wired World in their Hands

Peter Berger has pointed out that people in pre-industrial societies, in contrast to today, lived in a world surrounded by a 'sacred canopy'. [2] In other words, they took for granted that the realm of the spirit was very real, it hovered over them and had to be taken into account on a day-to-day basis. But that covering is no longer in place. It has been replaced by many smaller roofs of our own construction, or, to change the metaphor, the one Story which gave our ancestors their sense of identity has been replaced by many other stories. Among the latter are to be found the Human Rights Story, the Consumer-Society Story, the Multinational Corporation Story, the Do-Your-Own-Thing Story, the Gay/Lesbian Story, the Mass-Media Story, the New Age Story and so on.

In earlier pre-Enlightenment days the Christian story in the West had almost a clear run in what was mainly an oral society. It was one in which only the favoured few could read and write, and so the written word was not accessible to the vast majority. As a result the written Story was in the hands of a privileged minority, and among them were some of the clergy with a vested interest in keeping things as they were, according to their own reading of the Story. But when the move came, via the printing press and the related increase in literacy, from this oral society to a literary one, the uniqueness of the narrative by which people had up until then measured their lives was under threat. It meant that other narratives could now have a hearing, and this is precisely what began to happen. This has now become an even more general fact of life through the progression from a literary culture into an electronic one. The power of the modern image-makers is awesome in ways that need no documentation here. Modern iconography seduces young and old alike in spectacular fashion. It has been processed through television, the video, the computer, the CD-ROM and the silicon chip, the latter having done for electronic culture what the printing press did for the literary one. It has had both good and not so good effects.

On the positive side it seems to be at least an advance on the passive world of television audiences and the proverbial 'couch potatoes'. I feel far less snobbish about it than I used to, now that I have finally purchased a machine that does much more than my former word-processor could ever accomplish. And as for email, how did I ever survive without it?

---

2   Peter Berger: The Sacred Canopy: Elements of a Sociological Theory of Religion; New York, Doubleday, 1967

But none of us knows whether the information superhighway is good in itself, and we certainly cannot tell if the majority of the world's people will ever have access to it. Since 60% of the world's population have never made or received a telephone call, this seems unlikely for a long time to come. The former British Telecom advert announced that 'it's good to talk'. But modern technology can also drive people apart.

This, however, is the world within which the Church has the task of communicating the Christian story and of shaping and re-shaping its ways of worship. But we have to be careful, even in the church, of a creeping amnesia among us where the Gospel narrative is concerned. In the not too distant past in Britain, and in the United States for that matter, you could rely on a congregation's intelligent reception of preaching because the people in the pew possessed an appreciable biblical knowledge and felt reasonably at home with it. In my father's first church, in a rural setting in the 1930s, he could make assumptions about the biblical literacy of his congregation which no preacher could possibly make today. He preached without notes and so occasionally stumbled over a biblical quotation, but there was always someone at the door to correct him afterwards – and on one occasion actually shouted it out during the sermon itself!

But an overview of scripture is increasingly lacking among many of the members of our main-stream churches today. Elizabeth Achtemeier has written of the alarming indifference toward the Bible in certain protestant circles in the USA, and of which I have had some personal experience:

'It is now possible .... to carry on the expected work of a Protestant congregation with no reference to the Bible whatsoever. The worship services of the church can be divorced from Biblical models and become the celebration of the congregation's life together and of its more or less vaguely held common beliefs in some god. Folk songs, expressive of American culture, can replace the psalms of the church. Art forms and aesthetic experiences can be used as substitutes for communion with God. The preacher's opinions or ethical views can be made replacements for the word from the Biblical text. The sacraments can be turned into expressions of simply the congregation's fellowship together. But the amazing thing is that no one in the pew on Sunday morning may notice. Indeed, such a worship service may win praise from some quarters as "contemporary" and "relevant".' [3] During the years that have passed since she wrote those words, things have not got better; they have got decidedly worse! I do not think this situation has been replicated to the same extent in Britain, but the signs are not good.

Professor Horace Allen, decrying how present day worship has lost so many connections with its story, writes:
'Small wonder therefore that in our day, when society is becoming a violent shambles and a mere skeleton of a community, our forgetful churches, whose historic [liturgical] forms were given us to secure and form faith, are now losing out to secularism, cynicism and individualistically oriented spiritualities; charismatically preoccupied assemblies with their collapse of intentional form into mindless repetition; or that final indignity to the assembled, committed local community, the living–room presence of neither word, sacrament, prayer or praise, but the domination of demanding religious, even "evangelistic", entertainers.' [4]

In the same essay Professor Allen stresses that faith 'takes' liturgical shape, which in turn will inevitably shape that faith. I believe that the recovery of liturgical shape is essential if the Reformed church is to get back on track, especially where its biblical foundation is concerned, and to rediscover the good things in our heritage on the way. It may not be as difficult as we may think. We have to realise that, however varied the liturgical experiences of the universal church through its twenty centuries, there are actually only a few basic forms or structures of worship, and they have to do with sequence, setting, and sensory participation. All these forms are essential to a well-formed communal faithfulness, as we shall see later. What, then, is so special about the worship tradition out of which the Reformed churches have come? Indeed, what is so important about tradition in the first place? Surely it is the future which should monopolise our current thinking and planning? At least that is how the majority of the citizens of the West seem to view things today.

---

3   Elizabeth Achtemeier: The Old Testament and the Proclamation of the Gospel. Philadelphia, Westminster Press, 1973, p13.

4   Horace T Allen Jun: Liturgy as the Form of Faith; chapter 1 in the symposium: The Landscape of Praise; Pennsylvania Trinity Press International, 1996, p10.

Chapter Three

A Great Leap Backwards

A Great Leap Backwards

Soon after I retired, I presided at worship in a church where the order of service was less structured than the one to which I was accustomed. The minister, however, had given me *carte blanche* to change it if I so wished. It was an invitation I never extended to visiting ministers in my own church and would have thought it a discourtesy if they had done so, but I took him at his word. The changes were not drastic and there were no complaints afterwards – to my face that is. But at the door, as I was bidding farewell to the congregation, three people separately said, in almost identical terms, 'It was so good to have an old-fashioned service once again'. I quavered in reply: 'Don't you mean "traditional"?' To my relief they all agreed that that was indeed what they really meant. This has been an experience which has been repeated on several occasions.

Such people are representative of many others today who feel they are being short-changed in the sanctuary. They are not able to articulate a satisfactory explanation why they react this way and loyalty often constrains them from verbalising their sense of unease. They do not belong, for the most part, to the 'only-the-past-was-good-enough' brigade, but they do not like what seems to be a significant break from the traditions of the past. It is to their great credit that many of them do make a considerable effort to fall into line but it is not easy for them.

Richard Neuhaus writes: 'Christian ministers are strangely troubled by doing the "traditional" thing in worship. With respect to lesser traditions, people have little difficulty in recognising their responsibility to sustain and advance a particular history. It is hard to imagine some one in physics, for example, feeling uncomfortable with the claim that his or her responsibility is to sustain and advance the tradition of Thales, Kepler, Newton, Millikan, Bohr, and Einstein. It is likewise inconceivable that an actor would be insulted by the suggestion that he is in the tradition of Euripides, Shakespeare, Sarah Bernhardt and Charlie Chaplin. Yet one regularly encounters Christian ministers asserting their creativity in terms of their independence from the Christian tradition. In truth, what they often mean by "the traditional way" is the limited tradition of a particular denomination or even a local church. But liberation from much smaller and stifling tradition is precisely to be found in becoming more traditional. If we are to be free we must accept our responsibility as heirs of the many and diverse histories that make up the Christian tradition. The greatness of that tradition should be articulated and reflected in liturgy.' [1]

It is my contention that many of those churches today which regard themselves as in direct line to the sixteenth century Reformation are not fully accepting their responsibility as its heirs, especially where liturgy is concerned. Of course we must be open to change, change in the confidence of the promised guidance of the Holy Spirit, and our worship must have a contemporary tone to it without, at the same time, selling the pass to the craving for relevance above all else. (See chapter 17). There is a place for both recovery and reform as well as reform and change. This is the only way to be true to the Reformation claim: 'Ecclesia reformata, semper reformanda' – the church reformed, always in need of being reformed.

W D Maxwell wrote: 'It was not the intention of the Reformers to depart from the central tradition of Christendom and innovate according to mere whim or mood. Rather they counted themselves as the faithful trustees of catholic tradition, and if they simplified the Roman worship of their day they did so with the intention of removing all medieval and sacerdotal accretions in order to achieve the simplicity and purity of the primitive rites.' [2]

In lighter vein, an analogy from the wine industry may serve to reinforce the above. A few years ago the French wine industry was doing rather well. But there was a deepening concern that the growing dependence on foreign sales would prove destructive. The three-day festival in Beaune – *'Les trois glorieuses de Bourgogne'* – is always a joyful occasion, (don't ask me how I know!), what with sampling tents for wines and cheeses and charcuterie, and with street performers

1. Richard John Neuhaus: Freedom in Ministry; Grand Rapids, Michigan, William B Eerdmans Publishing Company, Revised Edition 1992, p148
2   W D Maxwell: John Knox's Genevan Service Book, 1556; Oliver Boyd, 1931, pp34-5

in medieval garb and all manner of competitions. But, beneath the surface jollity, there was anxiety. In Bordeaux, the great rival to Burgundy, a controversy raged (and still does) about the coarsening impact of American tastes, and especially the judgements of the US wine guru Robert Parker. It was alleged that some châteaux had abandoned the 'subtlety' of French tradition for a more 'vigorous' type of wine which appeals to America (that is, Parker). This was defined by one French critic as something which 'strikes the palate like a dollop of wine jam.'

Pierre-Henry Gagey, at that time the president of the Beaune wine traders, said that such antics would never be accepted in Burgundy: 'A great wine must remain faithful to its *terroir* [locality/origins]. The method of manufacture must express the qualities of the *terroir*, not blot them out'. I would suggest that something of the same applies to the liturgy of the Church!

We have, however, a problem. It is all very well writing and talking about the recovery of Reformed worship and its '*terroir*', never mind claiming for it a bouquet strong enough to arouse interest today, but what was it in the first place?

The term 'Reformation', as we have seen, is itself a blanket title which covers that movement in Western Europe which was concerned with the reform of the church of the day, a reformation in the moral, theological and institutional sense. The names of Martin Luther, Huldrych Zwingli and John Calvin are the names that immediately come to mind, but there were many more. Alister McGrath distinguishes four elements which can be identified in defining the term 'Reformation'. They are: Lutheranism; the Reformed Church, often referred to as 'Calvinism'; the 'radical Reformation' or 'Anabaptism'; and the 'Counter-Reformation' or 'Catholic Reformation'. He points out that, in the broadest sense, the term 'Reformation' is used to refer to all four movements. [3]

While recognising the strategic importance of Lutheranism in any discussion of the Reformation, it falls outside our immediate terms of reference as does, for obvious reasons, the Catholic Reformation, though, since Vatican II, the liturgy of many a Roman Catholic Church sometimes appears to be more in the spirit of

---

3   Alister E McGrath: Christian Theology – an Introduction; Oxford, Blackwell, 1994, pp62-3

the Reformation than it does in some of those who claim to be its direct heirs. So much so that, at the time of writing, there are those among the Curia who are trying to put the clock back somewhat. I hope they don't succeed!

As for the 'radical' Reformation or 'Anabaptist' strand, this today is represented more faithfully by those churches which often call themselves 'Free' and are identified accordingly by a 'free-er' approach to worship. Many of our charismatic and pentecostal churches, Baptists and even some Anglicans, fall into this category. This leaves us with Calvinism, and it is this strand which is our concern.

Of course the very name 'Calvin' immediately conjures up the great teacher's views on predestination, double predestination and the atonement with which even many within this tradition have a quarrel, to say the least. But, 'although it is often suggested that predestination stands at the centre of Calvin's system, this is not the case; the only principle which seems to govern Calvin's organisation of his theological system is a concern to be faithful to Scripture on the one hand, and to achieve maximum clarity of presentation on the other .... . Calvinism is still one of the most potent and significant intellectual movements in human history.' [4]

But despite this accolade, by the time of the late nineteenth and early twentieth century British and North American Presbyterianism (to take an example from a branch of Protestantism which traditionally has been looked upon as closest to Calvinism) had already lost much of Calvin's liturgical programme, such as singing the Psalms, weekly Lord's Supper, 'continuous' reading and preaching the Bible (chapter-by-chapter, week-by-week), the use of printed (*sic*) prayers and books, and the observance of the great festivals of Christmas, Easter and Pentecost. American Protestantism in particular had been overtaken first by a severe Puritanism and then by pietistic and evangelistic and charismatic reactions. These tendencies have also gradually become more pronounced in the UK and continue to increase.

It is not my business to criticise these movements too much. To do so would be to fail to recognise both that without them the present state of the Western Church would be even more parlous than it is, and also that we have much to gain

---

4   Ibid., p70

from the experience of fellow christians whose approach to worship is different from ours. Nonetheless I do have a certain amount of disquiet on this score. It is my contention that without a 'hard' liturgical core at the centre of all our worship, one which takes seriously the vital importance of an ordered liturgy with roots in the past, though not being closed off to new forms and 'experiments' in worship, we will be guilty of short-changing many of the faithful.

So our thesis finally emerges. The worship of Reformed (that is Calvinist) churches throughout the world at the beginning of the third millennium is in great need of reform and renewal if it is to serve the present day. This must be undertaken on the basis of that radical theology which has undergirded the Reformed Church and the liturgical programme advocated by John Calvin and his French and Swiss colleagues in the sixteenth century, but never fully achieved by the Reformed churches in later centuries. The outstanding example of the latter is Calvin's strong wish that Word and Sacrament should be conjoined on a weekly basis, but this has rarely taken place.

In justifying his views Calvin drew heavily upon the Scriptures but also on patristic scholarship, thereby demonstrating his own respect for tradition. Early church fathers, such as Justin Martyr, Irenaeus of Lyons, Origen, Tertullian, Athanasius and Augustine of Hippo are the main names that come to mind when thinking about this formative period in the development of Christian doctrine.

Calvin attempted to leap back over a thousand years of what he considered to be a millennium of stagnation where the theology and worship of the church were concerned. Just as he made this attempt, with some success, we will take a corresponding leap back to Calvin to see if we can benefit from his labours, even though what he discovered was, in its turn, never fully put into practice in his own day or since.

The two aspects of his teaching which concern us are those relating to the ministry and liturgy of the Church. These are closely linked, as we shall see later, and we shall also note the emphasis Calvin put on the holiness and sovereignty of God. These were the attributes which conditioned his understanding of what worship and ministry really are, and his insights provide our starting point as well.

Chapter Four

The Church's
Secret Treasure

The Church's Secret Treasure

Johnny was a Bristol gang-leader in the 1960s when I was a minister in that city. Nonetheless he had agreed to play a role in our modern rock passion play, *A Man Dies,*[1] which hit the national and international headlines at that time and was performed on national television and at the Albert Hall. Its first major public performance was in the Colston Hall, the West Country's premier concert hall in Bristol.

The cast arrived there early one evening for the dress rehearsal only to find that the Hallé Orchestra, under John Barbirolli, was still rehearsing for the following day's concert. The majority of the youngsters were happy enough to escape to the Green Room for refreshments and to annoy the musicians who were not needed on stage for the run-through of a Mozart symphony. But Johnny, staying with me in the balcony, leaned precariously over the rail; my peripheral view confirmed that he was enthralled by what was going on. After a while he sat back and enquired sadly: 'Why didn't no one before tell me it was like this?', and then returned his total attention to the platform. That was the beginning of Johnny's conversion to, and passion for, classical music; such was the effect of a chance encounter with it. Worship at its best can have a similar effect.

In the 1960s I took youngsters to Taizé and Iona, men and women for whom worship had not had a place in their lives before. But, with some of them, all this altered after they were exposed to what those two communities had on offer, at that time, in their respective sanctuaries.

Authentic worship has often aroused a positive response, similar in quality to that which the music had done where Johnny was concerned, in those who have strayed within its orbit for the first time. This, of course, is an observation that will seem preposterous to many today. The word that is frequently used by those who have 'given it a go' and been disappointed with the experience, especially the

---

1   Marvin and Hooper: A Man Dies, Darton, Longman and Todd, London, 1964.

young, is 'Boring!'. But time and again, in the history of the church, the liturgy has proved to be a converting ordinance as well as an edifying one, as Calvin always claimed it could be. Whether it has been the experience of corporate worship in a large company where hymns have been sung with conviction and where the Word read and preached has struck home, and the mystery of the Sacrament exerted its own fascination; whether it has been the experience of a small number gathered around a simple table breaking bread together; or whether it has been 'high' or 'low', the liturgy has succeeded again and again in drawing people into itself and out of themselves, so that their reaction has been anything but one of boredom, and their response, in many cases, has been akin to: 'Why didn't no one before tell me it was like this?'

We overlook at our peril the evangelical and missionary potential which is latent within the liturgy. This is why it is so vital to get it 'right', not least for our own sakes; we who 'whisper-it-not', if we were really honest, would confess that we too have found it boring more times than we care to remember.

Of course the validity of church worship does not stand or fall by the absence or presence of the boredom factor. In the popular BBC comedy series of the Seventies, *Yes, Minister*, the mandarin, Sir Humphrey Appleby, congratulates one of his underlings at the Foreign Office for the speech he had delivered at the White House to assembled diplomats on the subject of the British Civil Service. Afterwards Bernard, the Prime Minister's Private Secretary, queries the fulsome praise: 'But, Sir Humphrey, didn't you think that what he said was perhaps just a little bit boring?'

'Boring? Boring?' came the barked reply: 'Of course it was boring, but that's not the point. What do you think we are? Entertainers?'

It will always be the case that worship for some will be 'boring' simply because it deals with matters and concepts totally outside their present experience or immediate interest. That some are bored by it does not invalidate it, just as a Mozart symphony is not invalidated because many would be bored by it. We must take this into account before we concentrate on making our acts of worship more 'entertaining' and user-friendly. Also we must not feel too much shame that we, when participating in worship, do ourselves succumb to the boredom factor from time to time. But that does not alter the fact that we prefer to stick with the forms that we believe are valid, and, for that matter, consonant with Scripture. These are the reading and preaching of the Word, prayer, singing of praise, and the administration of the sacraments. We all simply go through the motions from time to time. This, paradoxically, can include our charismatic sisters and brothers too. 'Paradoxically', for, to all outward appearances, they seem anything but mechanical in their style of worship. But their 'style' can also involve much repetition, something they are at pains to decry in our more traditional forms.

All this is not to suggest that liturgical tradition – the way things have been done in the past – is above reproach; the Church always has need of her liturgical reformers. Occasionally there is need for big reforms, as in the sixteenth century and after Vatican II in the twentieth century. More limited, but needed, reforms also take place from time to time as the Reformation dictum, '*Ecclesia reformata, semper reformanda*' recognized: '*The Church reformed, always in need of being reformed.*' Nonetheless it is important to note that most of the sixteenth century Reformers were interested in reforming and purifying the liturgical forms they had already inherited from the medieval Roman Catholic Church, not in simply destroying or rejecting them out of hand. Their concern was to give worship back to the people by encouraging full, active and intelligent participation, especially at the sacraments. Thus their concern was to restore congregational singing, principally the Psalms in metrical vernacular translations (though Zwingli would not even go this far), and to provide for reading and preaching of the Bible sequentially as fully as possible in their own language. John Calvin asserted that all proper Lord's Day worship should include 'Prayer, the Word, the Table and Alms-giving.' That was a radical proposal in his day and it still is in ours.

But all this is exactly what contemporary liturgical renewal is striving to be about, just as it was both in the sixteenth century and in the aftermath of Vatican II. Since its inception the church had made its way into its surrounding cultures with a story the like of which people had never heard before. It was a story that was at one and the same time both a sacrifice of praise and a catechism, that is adoration accompanied by teaching. The Reformers stressed this priority of adoration in worship, arising out of their appreciation of the absolute holiness of

God: 'The greatest single contribution which the Reformed liturgical heritage can make to contemporary Protestantism is its sense of the majesty and sovereignty of God, its sense of reverence, of simple dignity, its conviction that worship must above all serve the praise of God.' [2] This emphasis can be made within the larger assembly in a church building, and by the small group in a room. That both today increasingly fail to do so in the attempt to be popular and relevant is occasion for deep sadness. The seekers after faith deserve more from us. We must be prepared to keep our nerve better than we do and not make too many concessions to the ongoing 'dumbing-down' process which is all too prevalent in our society today. This necessitates a closer look at what is actually going on in our churches on Sunday, questioning how valid or otherwise our practices are, and seeking to divest ourselves of distortions and distractions.

We have to acknowledge that our pre-packaged, programmed, bureaucracy-ridden and media-dominated consumerist society is no friend to spontaneous communities of like-minded souls. At our best we are one of the last 'live acts' going and it is the weekly worship which should focus it all, not on ourselves, but in adoration on Another, who finally 'calls the shots', whatever our own preferences and agendas. The church's secret treasure is not its budget but its worship. That is exactly what the Russian Orthodox Church at its best has always known, and what brought it through seven whole decades of atheistic oppression. Foolishly, its secular overseers, the government of the then Soviet Union, permitted it only its worship; but that, of course, was all it needed to survive.

Our worship is our treasure, our peculiar witness to a world long since bored with itself and manipulated by its worst and noisiest elements. This is why what we make of this treasure is crucial.

Our particular concern is the worship in those churches which today still consider themselves part of the Reformed heritage (although I hope that what is said is of relevance to other Christians too), and the context of any consideration of worship in the Reformed Church must be its confession: 'I believe in the one holy catholic and apostolic church'. Worship is not just *an* activity of the church;

---

2   Hughes Oliphant Old: 'Worship'; Atlanta, John Knox Press, 1984, pp176-177.

there is an important and historically accepted sense in which worship is *the* activity of the church, the activity by which the visible church of Christ may be discerned on earth as it points away from itself to the promised rule of God. So it is that John Calvin, commenting on this very confession in Book Four of the Institutes of the Christian Religion, affirms that: 'Wherever we see the Word of God sincerely preached and heard, wherever we see the sacraments administered according to the institution of Christ, there we cannot have any doubt that the Church of God has some existence'. [3]

We must now make some attempt to discover how the Reformed churches can 'shape up' for Christ's sake, and make of their worship a better instrument for both the praise of the Triune God and for renewing our understanding of the missionary and evangelistic task which we face today.

---

3   John Calvin: Institutes of the Christian Religion; London. James Clark and Co., 1949, Book 4, chap 1, section 9.

Chapter Five

Order! Order!

Order! Order!

'What does he mean, daddy, when he says "Order! Order!" Is he in a shop?' So said the five-year old daughter of a colleague of mine while watching the BBC's live coverage of Prime Minister's Question Time from the House of Commons. The same programme is shown in the USA where it has a small, but dedicated, cult following. This was especially true in the Thatcher years, and the Speaker's frequent calls to order were received with much merriment among some of my American friends. They thought it quaint and redolent of old-time school days.

But the concept of order is not altogether unfamiliar today, accustomed as we are to so much legislation promulgated on behalf of 'Law and Order'. That there has to be such legislation in the first place is an acknowledgment that Society is not as orderly as we would like it to be. On the other hand, the presence of civil liberty groups, human right groups, and the like, indicates that sections of Society feel the need to be watch-dogs against too much imposed orderliness. There is always a tension between these two poles and a delicate balance has to be sought over and over again. It is a balance that the church also needs to strive after in its regular worship if it is to avoid the twin dangers of oppressive formalism on the one hand and *laissez-faire* licence on the other.

In the Reformed churches of the past a frequent warning was sounded, in regard to the liturgy, that everything had to be done 'decently and in order'. This phrase was not an invention of the Reformers; they got it from St Paul: 'But all things should be done decently and in order' (I Corinthians 14:40). In verse 33 of the same chapter he writes: 'For God is a God not of disorder but of peace'.

This comes at the end of a homily on worship. In a day when the ministry of Word and Sacrament had not emerged in any set form, Paul recognised the importance of the contributions to worship from the whole people of God. These covered a wide spectrum, involving speaking in tongues at one end and more measured offerings at the other. All were welcome, up to a point, but it is obvious from verses 23 to 33 that the apostle is deeply concerned that things do not get out of hand. A measure of disciplined control and decorum was vital if things were not to slip into chaos, thereby threatening the task of building up the fellowship in love. (see vv 3-5,12,17,26).

If Paul addressed our churches today, he would have a different target for his criticism. In his excellent popular commentary on First Corinthians, Professor Nigel Watson, while agreeing with the warnings Paul gives concerning disorderly worship, writes: '.... but it must not be forgotten that it was addressed to a community whose patterns of worship were radically different from those of most mainstream churches today. It is, in other words, directed precisely to a community whose worship had become chaotic. What would Paul have said to a community whose worship was cerebral to the point of being rigid, and totally dominated by the celebrant? We can be sure that his emphasis would have been very different from his emphasis in this chapter'[1].

Professor Watson's strictures are salutary and pertinent. My only harsh caveat would be to point out that many of our mainstream churches today not only remain cerebral in their approach to worship, but they are now disorderly cerebral with it! This may sound uncharitable but, in far too many experienced instances, it is not an inappropriate description.

Order for order's sake, however, is not the issue here. The contention is that whereas the Reformed Church of a generation or two ago was still putting an excessive emphasis upon it to the exclusion of any flexibility, not least where participation of the members was concerned, we have now gone too far the other way. This would not be so serious a matter if it were only a question of different kinds of worship more natural to a variety of temperaments, but there is more at stake than this. The danger is that we fail to recognise how important liturgical form is in giving shape to faith. An ancient expression stated: '*lex orandi, lex credendi*', which can be paraphrased as: 'the way you pray determines what you believe.'

---

1   Nigel Watson: The First Epistle to the Corinthians; London, Epworth Press, 1992, p153

In the liturgical experience of the universal church there are actually only a few basic forms or structures, consisting of sequence, setting and sensory participation. These can be listed as calendars (daily, weekly, annual, civil and human), Bible services, sacramental services and pastoral offices such as weddings and funerals. All of these 'forms' are essential to a well-formed communal faithfulness, and also require some level or other of ordered mutual participation and meeting. Even where in corporate worship people seem to pay very little direct attention to one another, most, if not all, would affirm the essential importance of the presence of all the others. Nor dare we forget the seriousness with which the early church orders such as the *Didache* speak of the need to include absent members in eucharistic participation. All such forms help to shape the faith.

But vast and historic traditions of Christian worship have, by reason of didactism, formalism, clericalism, loss of historical memory and triumphalism, actually destroyed the forms they inherited, including the vital relationship among these forms. Thus 'Easter' in one tradition or another lost its connection with Baptism, Eucharist or the Jewish Pascha. 'Sunday' has lost its connection with Resurrection-Day or Eucharist, (see chapter 6), and with serious, thoughtful and participated proclamation, (see chapter 14).

Worst of all, as has already been hinted but not yet highlighted, the classic norm of Word and Sacrament itself has hardly ever succeeded in being a lively, perceived unity of form. Until recently in many traditions, either the Sacrament has seemed an occasional and unnecessary 'addition' to the sermon, or the Sacrament seemed not truly to need a sermon; an attitude which still persists in some quarters.

In the Reformed tradition we have, on the whole, lost sight of the crucial importance of the weekly Word-Sacrament shape of liturgy and how it can speak strongly of the Incarnation. If indeed the Word became flesh and lived among us full of grace and truth (John 1:14), then surely the liturgical communal event of the Word on the Lord's Day demands a concrete, incarnational, fleshly expression as well as the words of scripture and sermon that presumably speak of the Word. And to understand the proper incarnational character of sacramental worship either in the Supper or in Baptism, it is essential to recall that, especially in Reformed sacramental theology, the incarnational expressiveness of the Supper does not rest simply in its use of things as such, (e.g. water, wine, bread, vessels) but in its use of essential human corporate action, i.e. eating and drinking together in the context of a festive meal. When the meal aspect is not apparent, then the form and content of the Sacrament is 'deficient'. (See chapter 8 page 62.)

A friend of mine was once the guest preacher at an English public ('private' in the USA) school where the Eucharist was celebrated immediately after the sermon. As he had a strategic seat in the sanctuary, he was able to hear things that most of those present could not. Two youngsters from the junior school were serving at the altar for the first time and were, understandably, nervous about what they had to do, and when it had to be done. The time came for the vessels to be brought by them from the credence table and given to the chaplain-priest. They looked at each other, hesitated, and then one whispered to my friend: 'Shall we get the food now, sir?' He told them that he thought it would be a good idea, and there was no further problem.

Afterwards in the sacristy, the chaplain asked him, within earshot of the two boys, what the nature of their conversation had been. Unsuspectingly, my friend told him; whereupon the chaplain turned and not gently chastised the boys, saying: 'You were not bringing up *food* – you were bringing up the holy vessels as part of the offertory to God'! But the boys, albeit unwittingly, had got it right.

Christianity is not in its sacramental life a mystery religion, but a Semitic one. Its sacramental roots do not lie in changing natural things into super-natural symbols (see chapter 8), but rather in investing the most ordinary and essential human social activities with covenantal truth. The 'meal' emphasis is central to the form and meaning of the eucharist, but when I was a boy such 'meals' were few and far between. When they occurred, however, they were often more like a banquet, and I did not feel particularly undernourished.

In the Church of Scotland of my childhood only ordained ministers presided; in addition the 'celebrations' were few and far between – sometimes only once or twice a year. The infrequency arose initially because of the shortage of ministers, and not for theological reasons. At the time of the Reformation there were only

270 ordained ministers in the whole of Scotland. There was also, of course, a reaction from the abuses surrounding the Latin Mass, which did not help matters. But the longer the gap between communion services continued, the more did this state of affairs encourage a truncated view of what the Sacrament was.

The story is told of a confrontation between Gladstone and Queen Victoria in which the High Anglican Prime Minister was reportedly gently upbraiding his sovereign for her apparent preference for the liturgy of the Church of Scotland over against that of the Church of England. Gladstone took up the matter of communion, wondering how Her Majesty could prefer a church where, as with Crathie Parish Church at Balmoral, there were then only two celebrations a year. His bewilderment was compounded by the knowledge that it was possible for Her Majesty's long summer vacation amidst the lochs and braes of Scotland to take place without the Sacrament being available at all.

Victoria replied – one cannot imagine with a smile – 'Are six months too long for anyone to prepare for the Table of our Lord?' Gladstone's response is unknown.

In a way Her Britannic Majesty had a point, one to which a number of believers north of the border in Britain would still ascribe (although things have changed a great deal in the last few years, not least because of the influence of the Iona Community). If the Sacrament is considered in entirely penitential terms, as the supreme service at which the sinner receives the forgiveness of his or her sins, then indeed six months, six years even, might not be long enough for us to prepare for it.

Among those who think this way, there are some who take it to its logical conclusion and say that they will never be worthy to partake of the bread and wine this side of eternity. Even to this day there are those who will only allow themselves to be baptised when they think they are at the point of death. Many of them are good, spiritual people but one thing they forget; the Sacrament is Christ's gift to us, and we cannot make that gift any better by abstaining from it. We shall see shortly that to go down this penitential route is to finish with a truncated understanding of what the Sacrament is.

But I well remember the strong impression left on me as a child by the way in which the communion was celebrated in my father's first church, a country parish called Wamphray in the lowlands of Scotland. Memory fails to recall whether the sacrament took place once or twice a year, (I suspect the former), but whenever it happened it certainly was an awesome occasion – how else could it have left such an impression on a child who must have been no older than five at that time?

Almost the whole parish would gather, and for many this entailed long journeys over difficult terrain in a day when hardly anyone had a car. Shepherds came down from the hills, farmers left their farms in the hands of hired help, and all would begin to assemble as early as the Friday evening. That evening would be given over to a pre-communion service of preparation, followed by another on the Saturday evening. In between times, socialising would take place and meals shared in the houses of those who lived in the village. Then on the Sunday all would crowd into the church, or spill over outside. Memory does play tricks, but I seem to recall endless sunny days during the time of the Sacrament Week-End.

After the sermon was preached (longish to say the least), the minister and elders – the former suitably robed and the latter in frock coats – would retire to gather the bread and the wine. Then the Psalm: 'All People that on earth do dwell' to the tune 'Old Hundreth' would be sung during the 'Great Entrance' as the procession into church was called (see chapter 12). By the end of the 'Entrance' the elements had been placed reverently on the table and all was seen to be prepared. The elders, with the minister in their midst, stood behind the table facing the people and the climax to the week-end began.

But all was not over when the service ended. Many stayed on for the service of thanksgiving, which was held in the early evening before they wended their way home in the gathering darkness or stayed over only to depart at first light of dawn. Perhaps the need for this additional service would not have arisen if thanksgiving had been more strongly emphasised in the communion service itself. I owe a great debt to this 'high' tradition. It was only later that I grew to understand what its limitations were.

Chapter Six

Sabbath, Supper and Sunday

Sabbath, Supper and Sunday

One week-end in the early 1960s two friends of mine were travelling to the Isle of Iona in the Western Highlands of Scotland. They had crossed by ferry from Oban to Craignure, on the Isle of Mull, and only had the last lap of the long journey to complete; this was by bus to Fionnphort, a two-hour drive to the opposite end of the Island. From there, like all pilgrims to Columba's Island, they had to board another ferry (in those days no more than a large rowing boat) to take them over the Sound of Mull for the final stages.

Unfortunately, they had arrived late at Craignure. The bus driver, as was the custom, had waited for the ferry but could not guarantee that the ferry-man at Fionnphort would do the same. At any other time in the week this would not have been cause for alarm as the ferry sailed regularly between the two islands. This, however, was late Saturday afternoon, the eve of the 'Sabbath'. If they missed the last boat that evening, there would not be another one until the Monday.

The driver went as fast as he dared on the then single, and very narrow, road, but by the time they arrived they were already ten minutes late. The ferry-man was on the jetty, but it was not clear if he was tying up his craft for the week-end or untying it for a final trip.

They ran towards him: 'Is there another ferry?', one cried anxiously. 'Och aye' came the reply, couched in a gentle Gaelic lilt, 'Dinnae wheeste yoursels'. ('Don't you worry'). 'Oh, wonderful! What time do you leave?' 'Monday morning', he said, without a smile. 'A guid nicht to yee'. ('Good night to you').

There are still places in the Highlands where the 'Sabbath', as Sunday is still called, is strictly observed. Indeed, on one of the islands, just before I began this chapter, an ambulance plane was refused permission to land to pick up a very sick man; it was the Sabbath, you see! When I was a boy, one of the hymns I did not like was one whose first two lines read:

'O what their joy and their glory must be,
Those endless Sabbaths the blessèd ones see!'

The writer obviously anticipated not only that heaven would be like the sabbaths of his day, but it would be even better! Although my own family was not over-strict where the first day of the week was concerned, there were enough restrictions to worry me when I sang that hymn. If this was all we had to look forward to but on a larger scale, then we might as well have as good a time as possible here and now; the after-life was going to be no fun at all.

How many of us have really grasped the fact that the weekly Lord's Day has nothing to do with the institution the Hebrew Bible calls the 'Sabbath'? Hastings Nichols writes: 'The Puritans generally, in contrast to the Reformers, ignored even the most basic festivals of the church calendar, but were fervent Sabbatarians, applying to the Lord's Day the Old Testament regulations for the Sabbath'[1]. Perhaps, socially and politically speaking, this was more of a necessity in seventeenth century England; it was the only way to counter the civil, public and morally objectionable sort of day Sunday had become. Nichols, however, overlooks the fact that some Puritans took a more relaxed attitude to Sabbath observance. Milton, for example, wrote colourful masques to be performed on the Sabbath. But the theological mistake, of course, was to weigh down the Lord's Day with the entire burden of the Mosaic law, and thereby lose sight of the crucial evangelical understanding that Christ is the fulfilment of the law, whose resurrection has already ushered in the eternal and great Sabbath rest, and given new content to it. Willy Rordorf, in his important study 'Sunday', puts the issue this way:

'Accordingly, in the early years of the Church, Sunday was not thought of as inheriting and continuing the tradition of the Jewish Sabbath. Sunday had quite different roots. Its significance lay in the Christian understanding of worship at the centre of which was Jesus, the 'Lord'. Right down to the fourth century the idea of rest played absolutely no part in the Christian Sunday. Christians, like everyone else, worked on that day: it would not have occurred to them to do otherwise. It was only when the Emperor Constantine the Great elevated Sunday to be the statutory day of

---

1   James Hastings Nichols: Corporate Worship in the Reformed Tradition; Philadelphia, Westminster Press, 1968, p100.

rest in the Roman Empire that Christians tried to give a theological basis to the rest from work on Sunday which was now demanded by the state: to this end they fell back on the sabbath commandment.' [2] Those early Christian 'roots' quite simply are to be found in the unanimous affirmation by the Gospels that that was the day of resurrection (Matthew 28:1ff; Mark 16:2; Luke 24:1; John 20:1,19): 'On the First Day the Lord rose. On this same day he appears to his followers, expounded to them the Scriptures, and eats and drinks with them. It is on the same day that he appears the following week. It is on the First Day that the Holy Spirit is given. The importance of the First Day does not cease with these events. We soon find the Christian community assembling on this day for preaching and the breaking of bread. On this day alms are collected.... . By the end of the first century, the theological basis of Sunday is complete.' [3]

Oscar Cullman writes: 'The Lord's Day of the first Christians was therefore a celebration of Christ's Resurrection. Each Lord's Day was an Easter Festival, since this was not yet confined to one single Sunday in the year. This meaning of Sunday is repeatedly forgotten today. We are dealing with a specifically Christian festival day, and the fact that it derives its meaning from Christ's resurrection gives us an important hint as to the basic Christian meaning of all gatherings of the primitive community for worship.' [4]

Cullman's contrasting of the weekly resurrection festival with the later annual one, which is so much more familiar to us, is important. Whereas we are accustomed to think of an annual commemoration as a historical reference to the distant past (and we are unconsciously driven this way because of the way we use Holy Week to dwell on the past events leading up to Easter), we must take seriously the fact that a weekly cycle (especially on the first or 'eighth' day) clearly looks ahead to a final future fulfilment. That is to say, an annual calendar is inevitably historical whereas a weekly calendar is more likely eschatological. Karl Barth picks up the power of this weekly First Day as he defines 'the time of the community': 'The time of the community is the time between the first parousia [coming] of Jesus Christ and the second .... . The community exists between His

---

2   Willy Rordorf: Sunday: The History of the Day of Rest and Worship in the Earliest Centuries of the Christian Church; London, SCM Press, 1968, pp296-7.

3   H Boone Porter: The Day of Light – the Biblical and Liturgical Meaning of Sunday; Greenwich, CT USA, The Seabury Press, 1966, pp17-18.

4   Oscar Cullmann: Early Christian Worship; tr. A Stewart Todd and James B Torrance; London, SCM Press, 1953, p11.

coming then as the risen One and this final coming. Its time is, therefore, this time between. Its movement is from direct vision to direct vision; and in this movement by His Holy Spirit He Himself is invisibly present as the living Head in the midst of it as His body.' [5]

Thus we could say – as suggested by Paul V Marshall, reversing current and conventional wisdom – that it is not the case that 'Sunday is a little Easter', but rather that 'Easter is a big Sunday'. [6] We must, however, bear in mind that in fact 'Lord's Day' is the better term for that day. And it follows from all this that the church's worship on that day must inevitably focus on the risen Lord who is 'invisibly present' (Barth) and therefore must include as its inevitable climax that repeated and commanded event by which the Church has always and everywhere celebrated that promised presence, the sacrament of the Lord's Supper. Rordorf suggests: 'The sermon alone is not able to build up the community. It provides the basis, the foundation on which the community may be built up. The Lord's Supper is the visible actualisation of communion with the Lord and with one another, and only the Lord's Supper can make possible the integration of the body of Christ and the common growth of this body.' [7]

Some would see this as a relegation of the sermon to a slightly more subsidiary role. This is not necessarily so. I believe it can stand in its own right and has a sacramental efficacy of its own. I agree, however, with the implications of his argument. But is it how our churches today regard the Supper? Is it in fact the church's 'visible actualisation of communion with the Lord and with one another'? Is it where we find a definitive celebration and experience of the resurrection of the Lord?

Certainly not in contemporary Reformed practice! It is not even always celebrated on Easter Day – the one Sunday of the year which is associated with resurrection. Further, the mode and mood of its celebration can often be ponderous and sombre rather than glad and rejoicing. Quite often the penitential emphasis will still outweigh that of thanksgiving.

---

5   Karl Barth: Church Dogmatics, 1V/1 The Doctrine of Reconciliation; tr. G W Bromiley; Edinburgh, T & T Clark, 1956, p725.

6   'Landscape of Praise' – Ed. Blair Meeks, Pennsylvania ,Trinity Press International, 1996, pp 39ff.

7   Rordorf: op.cit. p306.

The organist at one of the churches where I was the minister did an excellent job of work, but, at communion, when the vessels were being carried out of the sanctuary by the elders at the end of the service, his recessional music was always low-key and usually quite funereal in tone. One day I plucked up the courage to raise the issue with him (tactfully of course – good organists are hard to come by!). Why did he do it? He was astonished and replied: 'Because it is such a sad occasion. We are remembering the death of Jesus. You can't be happy about a death.'

This understanding is still quite common today and therefore, even if the preceding argument concerning the link between Lord's Day and the Lord's Supper was more widely embraced, that would certainly not in itself suggest the inevitability of its being 'celebrated' as such. Perhaps then the time has come to say, as lovingly as possible, with the Apostle Paul, 'When you come together, it is not really to eat the Lord's supper'. (I Corinthians 11:20).

Then what is it? The answer is: The Last Supper. Many of our services of communion are too often dominated by the Pauline 'words of institution', (so called), which have helped us lose sight both of the Messianic, eschatological emphasis found in the Didache (*c.* 90 CE) which never even mentions the *Last Supper*, and also of the resurrection references to eating and drinking in Luke 24, John 21, Acts 10:41, to say nothing of the ethical implications of the 'lost sacrament' of the foot-washing in John 13.

But now an awkward question arises: Why has this Lord's (i.e. Last) Supper always been celebrated on Sunday and not, as Rordorf trenchantly asks, 'on Thursday evening'? [8] (although he fails to mention Maundy Thursday). His answer is the conclusion 'that the meeting of the disciples with the risen Lord on Easter evening must have been for them like a second institution of the Lord's Supper,' and it was this Supper of, and with, the risen Lord (kyriakon deipnon), which finally gave a name to 'the first day of the week', namely: kyriake hemera. 'It seems probable' says Rordorf, 'that the whole day on which this "Lord's Supper" took place received the title the "Lord's Day".' [9]

---

8   Ibid., p233
9   Ibid., p221

Thus even the terminology of Day and Supper are intimately related such that the *Last* Supper functions only through the prism of the first day of the week. Therefore so long as we continue to celebrate the Lord's Day without the Lord's Supper (and thus to isolate the Supper from the Day), we are consenting in and encouraging the loss of the Lord's Day to that legalistic Sabbath so familiar to us in the days of our youth, and to the collapse of the Lord's Supper into a pre-resurrection Last Supper. If we continue so to view it, then even a monthly eucharistic schedule suffers from the same limitations as an annual or quarterly one. The indissoluble link of the Day and the Supper has not been made. If we are ever to seem different from a Christian synagogue, the 'Lord's Supper' must be reunited with the 'Lord's Day'. If we are ever to be better equipped to re-present the fullness of the Christian story to a world like ours, then we must make every effort to bring about this union and so to do it that the note of celebration is sounded loudly and clearly.

Chapter Seven

Celebration

Celebration

The organist mentioned in the previous chapter obviously did not think of the sacrament in terms of celebration even though on occasions he had played the hymn '*Deck thyself my soul with gladness*' at communion! Sadly he is not alone in this respect but, in the light of how some local churches 'celebrate' the Gospel story in their worship, his misunderstanding on this score is excusable. Perhaps he would not have made the same mistake if he had been exposed Sunday by Sunday to worship of a more charismatic timbre.

I think, however, that I represent a considerable number of Christians who are uncomfortable with, and not a little worried by, the worship on offer in churches which are often called 'charismatic', while, at the same time, having to recognise that the problem could be me! For it is obvious that such churches often succeed in presenting a style of worship which is vibrant and attractive (especially to the young) in contrast to what many consider to be the boringly formal style of more traditional worship as referred to in chapter four. Charismatics sound a more overt celebratory note in their assemblies which traditionalists seem to lack, and which proves to be very attractive. So why am I worried?

To be brutally frank, I am worried because the methods used in their attempt to bring the Gospel within everyone's reach often succeed in trivialising the faith. Why is it that many of them show such an antipathy towards the traditional ways in which the church has communicated the Gospel message? It is an antipathy which, in certain quarters, amounts almost to a total neglect of the prayers and hymns of the past (even the sacraments in some instances!) through which the Church has offered its worship to God.

The motivation behind this is all too often the desire to make worship so user-friendly that it will have maximum appeal – especially to the outsider. But in such attempts to cast the net as widely as possible, a dumbing-down process can take place which only succeeds in leaving many of its adherents in a permanent stage of adolescence. This style of worship is characterized by the praise song – 'four words, three notes, and two hours', as it has been irreverently described – often with a mantra-like repetition of phrases from Scripture displayed using an overhead projector or video monitor.

Let me bring in Dr Hart of Westminster Theological Seminary, California, in the attempt to divert some of the flack that could otherwise fly directly to me!

'Gone are the hymnals that kept the faithful in touch with previous generations and saints. They were abandoned, in many cases, because they were filled with music and texts considered too boring, too doctrinal, and too restrained. What boomers and busters need instead .... is a steady diet of religious ballads, most of which date from the 1970s, the decade of disco, leisure suits, and long hair. Gone too are the traditional elements of Protestant worship: the invocation, the confession of sins, the Apostles' Creed, the Lord's Prayer, the doxology, and the Gloria Patri. Again, these elements are not sufficiently celebrative or "dynamic", the favourite word used to describe the new worship .... . And the substance of much preaching is more therapeutic than theological.' [1]

The mistake often made is to equate celebration with the state of happiness; hence those fixed smiles mentioned in the Introduction which can drive the rest of us crazy. But the former does not necessarily require the existence of the latter.

At funerals, for instance, most mourners would not be happy in the accepted sense, (or at least they would try not to look it even if they were!); but a Christian funeral service should sound a strong note of affirmation and hope, one which reminds the participants that an element of joy underpins the whole of the proceedings, albeit one which does not necessitate smiles all round. 'Celebration does not always mean jumping for joy nor is it always a festival of song and dance. It may include more inward and sober elements. It does, however, invariably contain the awareness that my acts have a deeper, more transcendent meaning than that which meets the eye, even though I may not be able to put this meaning into words.' [2]

---

1   D G Hart: Recovering Mother Kirk: The Case for Liturgy in the Reformed Tradition; Grand Rapids, Michigan, Baker Academic, Baker Book House Company, 2003, p82.

When, at the table, we hear the words 'Do this in remembrance of me' there is, of course, a recalling to mind the terrible events of those particular days which form a pivotal part of the whole story. At that precise moment we are remembering the sacrifice of Christ who came to earth and suffered for us, offering his life back to the Father in perfect obedience. It is such a special moment that Roman Catholics mark it with the ringing of the sanctuary bell. Maybe 'celebration' is not an adequate word to describe that particular moment in the liturgy's progression. It can, however, be quite legitimately applied to the eucharistic action as a whole. What confronts us there is not simply the death of Jesus, but the death of the Christ whom God raised from the dead and who is now present with us in the power of the Spirit. This is not a moment of nostalgia, as some of our worst hymns and ballads would have us believe; it is a moment for the exercise of an act of corporate memory which, through the preaching of the Word of promise, and under the elements of bread and wine, confronts us with the real presence of Christ, (see chapter 8). This is cause aplenty for celebration, but there is another reason why this is also the case.

> T S Eliot wrote:
> 'This is the use of memory:
> For liberation – not less of love but expanding
> Of love beyond desire, and so liberation
> From the future as well as the past.' [3]

Liberation from the future as well as the past is an insight based on Eliot's understanding of the eschatological thrust at the heart of the Gospel and witnessed to in the sacraments: 'For as often as you eat this bread and drink the cup, you proclaim the Lord's death *until he comes.*' (I Corinthians 11:26). Not only are we engaged in a dynamic act of memory which reminds us of God's saving work in the past, and which makes it a present reality sacramentally, but we are assured of the continuance of this work to liberate us, come what may, until that day when we will eat and drink with him in his kingdom. And so, as we eat and drink as he commanded us to do, we can legitimately call our action in the sanctuary 'celebratory' – of past, present and future – a 'Eucharist', which is 'Thanksgiving' for our unity and liberation in Christ.

---

2   Raimund Panikkar: The Vedic Experience; London, Darton, Longman and Todd, 1977, p36; quoted by A M Allchin: The Dynamic of Tradition; London, Darton, Longman and Todd, 1981, pp104-105.

3   T S Eliot: The Four Quartets, Section 3; London, Faber and Faber, 1959, lines 156-168.

History and hope are no strangers to one another in the Bible. It speaks of an old covenant and a new one. The sacrament of the Supper remembers something old and anticipates something new. Christ Jesus is Alpha and Omega, beginning and end. It should be no surprise therefore that the Church, which is the people of the Bible and the body of Christ, is always moving back and forth between the new and the old. That is exactly what the Reformation of the sixteenth century was all about, and that is also exactly what it means to be a reformed and reforming church today.

All this must be what drives the liturgy and makes of it both a converting and edifying ordinance. The means of grace are readily at hand within its contours – the prayers, the readings from Scripture, the preaching of the Word, and the sacraments. The liturgy must not be used primarily as a means of reaching the outsider – that is not its purpose at all. It stands in its own rite (*sic*), differing from the primary aim of many christian assemblies today, which appears to be to reach the lost and the uncommitted. Of course there is a place for this but: 'Once the gathering of the saints and the proclamation of the Word become chiefly a way to reach the lost, worship moves from its properly God-centred orientation to one in which pleasing men and women, preferably the lost (or in today's lingo, "seekers"), becomes the overarching goal.' 4

All this is not to imply a detachment from the concerns of the world or our mission to the world; the very opposite in fact.

On the Sunday following the September 11th terrorist attack on the Twin Towers, I went to church as usual. Faces were sombre, people were outraged and we were certainly not at all happy. Nonetheless, what we engaged in was still a celebration and to describe it as such is not to suggest a callous indifference towards those terrible events.

It was a relief to let the liturgy wash around us and uphold us in a way in which it would have been impossible for any sermon to do on its own. The story was re-enacted, reminding us once again of our creation, redemption and eternal destiny. Our solemn demeanour was understandable, but the mood did not signify a final despair with the human situation. We were not there, à la Dostoevsky,

---

4   D G Hart: op.cit p212

wanting to give back our entrance ticket. The sermon and the worship took full cognisance of the depravity in the world, but the words and actions of the whole service were an unction, an anointing, a means of grace, a reminder of the victory already won over the powers of darkness, albeit one yet to be fully consummated. We were indeed, like Paul, knocked down but not knocked out. At no point were we left with the feeling that this evil happening did not concern us, or that it, and others like it, would have the last word.

Richard Neuhaus observes how he has noticed over the years, in the inner cities of America, many burned-out cases among people, young and old, who set out with admirable dedication to make a difference for the better to people's lives, but finally the evidence of futility exhausted that devotion and broke that determination. He remarks wryly that Brooklyn and the South Bronx, and their counterparts in Cleveland, St Louis, Chicago and Los Angeles, do not deal kindly with those who would change the world for the better. He points to that process which many of us have witnessed, in one degree or another, of people abandoning ministries, shattered by a sense of guilt and betrayal; of people accepting more comfortable positions as an admission of defeat, even of people turning to suicide. He adds as a generalisation but one which, nevertheless, we must take on board: 'Where the most difficult ministries are sustained, where ministries are least likely to be accompanied by the criterion of success, endurance is empowered by the sacramental anticipation of transcendent hope.' [5]

Of course we do not always go to communion in the aftermath of a great tragedy or some shattering incident in our world. Most of us wend our way to church on a Sunday morning after a week of quite ordinary days, both domestically and within the larger community. But many a Sunday congregation will have in its midst those for whom the week has been a sad one. There will be at least one heavily burdened soul present, probably more, for whom the preliminary cheery 'good-morning' may only serve to compound their sadness or despair. Here again, the sheer 'objectivity' of the Sacrament, preceded by the preaching of the word of promise, must be allowed to do its work without recourse to false *bonhomie* or inconsequential chattiness or appeals for conversion.

---

5   Richard Neuhaus: op.cit p109

But all this is not the full story where the Lord's Supper is concerned. So far the emphasis has been on the place of celebratory memory within the context of the meal. Only oblique mention has been made concerning the 'Real Presence' and the notion of sacrifice, both of which categories have been in the forefront of liturgical debate over the centuries, not least at the Reformation. This must now be rectified, but in the process I hope to show that neither of these categories are matters for theoretical speculation but, rather, are highly relevant to the ongoing missionary and evangelical task of the church. They also provide additional reasons to justify describing the Eucharist as a 'celebration'.

Chapter Eight

Hocus Pocus

Hocus Pocus

Many priests prior to the Reformation were men of little education but they had a sufficient grounding in 'dog' Latin to enable them to get through the mass and the other offices at which they presided. But with a multiplicity of masses, and congregations which did not understand Latin anyway, speed was of the essence and incoherence often the result. At the consecration of the bread the Latin words were: 'Hoc est corpus meum' – 'this is my body' – but the more speedily they were said the more easily they sounded like 'hocus pocus'. The Reformers declared that this was precisely what it was anyway – mumbo jumbo, superstitious repetition, and based on a false theology into the bargain. But very soon they themselves had to come to terms with the teaching behind the 'hocus pocus', i.e. the doctrine of the real presence of Christ on the altar – 'transubstantiation', as it came to be called – and to work out where they stood on the matter. They discovered, however, that they were by no means united.

The three main Reformers in the eucharistic debate of those years were Luther, Zwingli and Calvin. At the Marburg Colloquy (1529) between the Lutherans and the Zwinglians, the fifteenth of the articles drawn up by Luther at its end admitted that the two parties had not been able to agree on whether the true body and blood of Christ are bodily in the bread and wine.

Lutherans, like the Roman Catholics, said that they were, but Zwingli said they were not. Calvin, who only appeared long after the Marburg debate, disagreed with both Luther and Zwingli, although he never denied that Christ was present in the sacrament.

For Calvin a sacrament was, first and foremost, an act of God rather than an initiative on the part of the communicant or the church: 'He was convinced that Zwingli was wrong about the principal agent in both Baptism and the Lord's Supper. A sacrament is first and foremost an act of God or Christ rather than of the candidate, the communicant, or the church; Zwingli had the priorities wrong. Indeed, he not only put first what can only be secondary but made it the whole sacrament; he imagined that a sacrament is only an act by which we attest our faith and not rather, as it truly is, a sign by which God strengthens our faith.' [1]

It has been the contention in these pages that the sixteenth century reformer most relevant and significant for the Reformed churches today is John Calvin, and nowhere is he more important for us than in his sacramental theology. Diarmaid MacCulloch writes: 'Typically, he [Calvin] returned to Augustine of Hippo, and like so many Reformers, was grateful for the crisp Augustinian definitions of the sacraments as "a visible sign of a sacred thing" or "a visible form of an invisible grace".' [2]

John Calvin argued that there was an intimate connection between a symbol and what it represented. The sign itself is, indeed, visible and physical, but what it conveys is invisible and spiritual. But the connection between them is so intimate that what is being signified depends closely on its sign: 'Believers ought always to live by this rule: whenever they see symbols appointed by the Lord, to think and be convinced that the truth of the thing signified is surely present there. For why should the Lord put in your hand the symbol of his body, unless it was to assure you that you really participate in it? And if it is true that a visible sign is given to us to seal the gift of an invisible thing, when we have received the symbol of the body, let us rest assured that the body itself is also given to us.' [3] In general Calvin believed that although ideas may be distinguished, they cannot be separated, and this had a great influence on his understanding of the nature of sacramental symbols.

En passant, and in lighter mood, some of us can appreciate a non-theological claim that Calvin makes:

---

1   B A Gerrish: Grace and Gratitude; Minneapolis, Augsburg Fortress, 1993, p8.
2   Diarmaid MacCulloch: Reformation – Europe's House Divided; London, Penguin Books, 2004, p250.
3   Institutes of the Christian Religion – tr. Henry Beveridge, London, James Clarke, 1949, Book 4, chapter 17, section 10, p564.

'When we see wine set forth as a symbol of blood, we must reflect upon the benefits which wine imparts to the human body .... . These benefits are to nourish, refresh, strengthen and gladden.' I am not sure how the Reformer's Puritan successors reacted to that, but it does help to correct somewhat our impression that Calvinism had a kill-joy approach to life. A reading of Book 3 chapter 10 section 2 will confirm that this was far from being the case. (In an American Southern Baptist Sunday School manual it was tortuously explained that when Paul advised Timothy to take a little wine for his stomach's sake, he was really meaning he had to rub it in!)

The '*Directory for Worship of the Westminster Assembly*' instructs the minister to pray God 'to vouchsafe his gracious presence, and the effectual working of his Spirit in us, and so to sanctify these Elements both of Bread and Wine, and to bless his own Ordinance, that we may receive by faith the Body and Blood of Jesus Christ crucified for us, and so to feed upon him, that he may be one with us and we with him, that he may live in us and we in him, and to him, who hath loved us, and given himself for us.' [4] All this, and more, underlined the central Calvinist emphasis on actual communion with the risen Lord, who was 'really' present with his people.

The above, however, has tended only to stress the role of the elements – a view sometimes referred to as 'Elementarianism' – but it is the concern of the whole rite, word and action, giving and receiving, and in the sharing fellowship that concerns us. But we must now look at that other category which has not been mentioned so far, that of sacrifice. Just as the doctrine of transubstantiation was closely linked to the Roman Catholic understanding of the priestly office, (only the priest could consecrate the elements and 'change' them by the power of the Spirit into the Body of Christ), so also was the notion of sacrifice.

The concept of sacrifice is one that modern Reformed church men and women seem to find distasteful, to say the least. This is a pity because, redefined, we can discover an understanding of it which could reinvigorate our worship and speak eloquently to our modern condition. As it happens, the Roman Catholic emphasis on the centrality of sacrifice was something I encountered at an early age.

---

4   The Westminster Confession of Faith: Of the Celebration of the Communion, or Sacrament of the Lord's Supper. p154.

After his early ministry in Scotland, my father was called to be a minister in the then Presbyterian Church of England. In the early 1940's we all moved to Blackburn in Lancashire. We lived in a large manse across the road from the church, which was always within view. Our next-door neighbours were Irish Roman Catholics, devout, and with eight children.

One Sunday morning after my mother, brother and I had returned from church, I went out to play in the large garden frontage which both houses shared. I was joined by Ned, the youngest of our neighbours' children and who had just returned from Mass. We were both about ten years old at the time.

During our play, Ned looked up and saw my robed father still talking to some late-departing members of the congregation at the door of the church. Pointing, he taunted: 'Your daddy can't bring Jesus Christ down into his church like our priests can bring him down onto our altars!' Such was my abrupt introduction to an ancient controversy at the heart of the Church's understanding of its ministry.

That particular encounter ended with a fist-fight in the rhododendron bushes, brought to an abrupt conclusion by the intervention of my mother. When, however, she learned the reason for the fisticuffs, (I had sobbed: 'You tell him that my daddy *can* bring Jesus Christ down into our church and he can do it better than his priests') she marched off, myself in tow, to confront Ned's mother. But Mrs Moriarty was not at all sympathetic: 'Well, Mrs Marvin', she replied 'What Ned said is quite true. Your husband certainly does not have the power that our priests have.' The families, thereafter, did not speak to each other for some considerable time; but such a disputation, on a wider canvas, has kept sections of the world-wide family of the church on non-speaking terms for much longer.

Now Ned was quite right as far as the official teaching of his church was concerned, and still is for that matter. The word 'priest', which derives from 'presbyter' but is more commonly associated with the Latin 'sacerdos', places a much greater emphasis on the mediating and cultic dimensions of the ministry of the individual – his 'power' – hence young Ned's stricture. The priest can do something on behalf of the people which the people cannot do for themselves.

This is emphasised especially when it comes to the priest's role at the offering of the eucharistic sacrifice on the altar, repeating there what Protestants claim that Christ accomplished once for all on Calvary, which, therefore, is unrepeatable. I was not to know at the time that, along with the priest's role as the exclusive purveyor of God's grace in forgiveness, these aspects of the priestly function in the mass were to Luther, Calvin and Zwingli the supreme abomination (*horrendae abominationis caput* – Calvini *Opera Selecta,* 1-152). But, even if I had known, I am sure Ned would not have been mightily impressed.

'Minister' in Reformed Church doctrine is understood as one who indeed has a specific role and presides at services of Word and Sacrament, but does so as the servant of the people of God and not as the intermediary on their behalf. But this is to anticipate chapter 13 on ministry and leadership in today's church. Our concern here is with the category of sacrifice and its role, or otherwise, in Reformed worship. It is only fair, however, first to recognise that the present day Roman Catholic understanding of the sacrifice offered by the priest on the altar does not appear to be quite so stark as it did at the time of the Reformers. Conversations in recent years between Anglicans and Roman Catholics have helped to 'soften' matters considerably.

'Christ's redeeming death and resurrection took place once and for all in history. Christ's death on the cross, the culmination of his whole life of obedience, was the one perfect and sufficient sacrifice for the sins of the world. There can be no repetition of or addition to what has been accomplished once and for all by Christ. Any attempt to express a nexus between the sacrifice of Christ and the eucharist must not obscure this fundamental fact of the Christian faith. Yet God has given the Eucharist to his church as a means through which the atoning work of Christ on the cross is proclaimed and made effective in the life of the church. The notion of 'memorial' as understood in the Passover celebration in the time of Christ – that is, the making effective of an event in the past – has opened the way to a clearer understanding of the relationship between Christ's sacrifice and the eucharist. The eucharistic memorial is no mere calling to mind of a past event or of its significance, but the church's effectual proclamation of God's mighty acts. Christ instituted the Eucharist as a memorial (anamnesis) of the totality of God's reconciling action in him. In the eucharistic prayer (see chapter 11), the Church continues to make a perpetual memorial of Christ's death, and its members, united with God and with one another, give thanks for all his mercies, entreat the benefits of his passion on behalf of the whole church, participate in those benefits and enter into the movement of his self-offering.' [5]

In some respects it is difficult to see in these words any problem for members of the reformed churches today. In fact they substantiate an important practice in our celebrations of the Lord's Supper, namely the corporate offering-up of the sacrifice of praise. There is also no hint of the medieval idea that the sacrifice of the mass pays a price to God that he himself is to receive as a satisfaction for our sins, that, in Calvin's words, 'Christ must be sacrificed every day to do us any good.' [6] For such an absence we must be truly thankful, but, as a Reformed Church minister, I have one important reservation.

I welcome ecumenical convergence on the idea of sacrifice in the Eucharist, but it cannot set aside Calvin's insistence that the Supper is a meal, not a sacrifice as such, and the table is not an altar. This is not to suggest that it is just a simple fellowship meal – that's where some churches get it wrong. We are not just remembering a meal in Jerusalem all those years ago or that death all those years ago. We are doing all that, of course, but doing it also as an Easter celebration: 'We are made "present to ourselves" as people complicit in the betrayal and death of Jesus and yet are still called and accepted, still "companions" of Christ in the strict sense – those who break bread with him.' [7]

Calvin, for all his vitriol against the mass, did not want to exclude sacrificial language from it altogether. There is, for instance, an important place for the sacrifice of praise which does not simply consist of the singing of hymns on Sunday (although they are an important part of it), but involves the offering of ourselves, in body, mind and spirit, to the One God, for his glory and service in the world. In addition the eucharistic sacrifice also meant for him:

---

5   Anglican-Roman Catholic Commission: Eucharistic Doctrine: in Final Report; London CTS/SPCK, 1989, pp13-14.
6   Calvin: op.cit 4,18. 7 (2: 1435-36)
7   Rowan Williams: Resurrection; London, Darton, Longman and Todd, 1982 edition, p40.

'.... whatever we do to worship God, including the duties of love; for when we embrace our brothers and sisters in love, we honour the Lord himself in his members. Kindness and sharing are offerings that please God; all the good works of believers are spiritual oblations (*hostiae*).' [8]

Calvin himself puts it thus: 'All these things finally depend on that larger sacrifice by which we are consecrated in body and soul as a holy temple to the Lord .... , so that everything in us may serve his glory and be filled with zeal to increase it.' [9]

Saint Paul was the precursor of this insight when he wrote: 'I appeal to you, therefore, brothers and sisters (*sic*), by the mercies of God, to present your bodies as a living sacrifice, holy and acceptable to God, which is your spiritual worship' (Romans 12:1).

Many a prayer at the offertory in a Reformed church has commenced with: 'All things come of thee and of thine own have we given thee,' but it is unfortunate that in Reformed church services these words are often simply associated with the money-offering; this has the effect of narrowing their application to it alone. Charles Wesley's hymn: 'O Thou who camest from above', redresses this and, sung at the end of a service, puts it all quite powerfully:

'.... Jesus, confirm my heart's desire
to work and speak and think for thee ....
Ready for all thy perfect will
my acts of faith and love repeat,
till death thine endless mercies seal
and *make my sacrifice complete*'.

The Lord's Supper provides the opportunity for widening the application of such words and to infuse the service with a more all-embracing note of sacrificial praise and thanksgiving in the context of the celebratory meal.

---

8   Gerrish: op.cit p155.
9   Calvin: op.cit. 4. 18. 16 (2:1444).

In the Protestant tradition, the response of the worshipper to God's action in Christ has often been conveyed through the sung word. Hymn-singing has played a vital role, indeed often dominating the liturgy – except for the sermon. So we need now to turn our attention to the place the hymn has had in Reformed services, and particularly in recent times.

Chapter Nine

The Hymn Sandwich

The Hymn Sandwich

When we think of hymns, the phrase 'hymn-sandwich' may come to mind. This is the term that, on the one hand, can be used to typify those acts of public worship which are devoid of shape and movement, a mishmash of prayers, readings, preachings (the 'fillings') loosely bound together by a number of unrelated hymns/songs (the 'bread'). This is the kind of worship that owes nothing to our Reformed ethos, but which, sadly, is not uncommon today.

On the other hand, however, the 'hymn-sandwich' at its best has not always been the formless entity that many of its critics have assumed it to be. There was often a shape and progression to it which did not always occur out of sheer happenstance and which reflected something of the true dynamic of Reformed worship and, happily, has not died out altogether.

Such services commenced with the 'Call to Worship', usually incorporating a scriptural injunction focusing on the sovereignty and majesty of God. This was followed by the first hymn, appropriately one of adoration and praise. After this introduction came the first prayer which continued the theme of adoration. This cumulative acknowledgment of the holiness of God then served, by comparison, to remind the people of the frailty and sinfulness of our nature. Thus the mood of adoration phased into confession, followed by the pronouncing of the Gospel word of pardon. This section concluded with an invocation of the Holy Spirit, asking that the Spirit's presence would enable the congregation to make a fitting offering of their worship at the throne of grace and to renew them in body, mind and spirit.

Thereafter the first scripture lesson was read, usually a passage from the Hebrew Scriptures, or Old Testament as it is still often called. This was a reminder that our roots go back long before Christ, to the time of Abraham and Isaac and Jeremiah and David and all the rest, among whom God was also at work. In the early Christian writings it is quite striking how the way in which the great figures of the history of Israel, Abraham and Moses, David and Elijah seem to be alive within the memory of the Church and we have a responsibility to maintain that memory through the liturgy in which we engage. The Old Testament is, among other things, what provides the setting for the New and to omit it from a full act of worship is not to be encouraged. Doing so can only serve to further our growing amnesia where our elder brothers and sisters, the Jews, are concerned.

'It was Calvin who opposed the traditional and commonly accepted assumption of the rejection of Israel. What he did say in this regard deserves the utmost attention and has wide-ranging significance for the Christian-Jewish dialogue, begun amongst us in recent decades'. [1]

After the lesson from the Hebrew scriptures, a talk was usually given to the children (see chapter 15), prior to their departure for the Junior Church or Sunday School. Thereafter a hymn or, more likely, a psalm would be sung (often a metrical one, but not always). This was in accord with the ancient liturgical tradition wherein what was known as the 'gradual' was sung at this point. In the Western Church this consisted of a set of antiphons (something sung responsively), mainly from the psalms, and was placed immediately after the Old Testament lesson. The word comes from the latin '*gradus*' meaning a 'step', and it has its origin in the custom of singing it on the altar steps. The gradual psalm also represented a step-like progression from the Old Covenant to the world of the New.

After the Psalm there was an immediate move into the world of the New Covenant and the reading of the Epistle came first, as it always should. As well as consisting of documents that pre-date the gospels, the epistles were written with particular situations and problems in mind which concerned the Christian churches in their early years. They were not written primarily as careful expositions of the Gospel but addressed, sometimes passionately, day-to-day occurrences and crises in the local church to which they were sent.

---

1   Hans-Joachim Kraus: Toward the Future of Reformed Theology; Editors David Willis and Michael Welker; Grand Rapids, Michigan. Eerdmans Publishing Company, 1998, p327

It is right and proper that we remember in our assemblies these earlier struggles, ones in which we see a reflection of some of our own, and learn, one would hope, to take the writers' teachings, admonitions and encouragements to our own hearts. But because of the reasons given above, the epistle should take second place to the Gospel reading of the Good News, as it always did in the traditional 'hymn-sandwich'. The Gospel is the climax to the whole story; it is what gives rise to our faith in the first place and must not be relegated to an earlier position in the service. Sadly, for reasons I can never begin to fathom, it suffers such demotion in many of our services today. An entirely inadequate explanation given by some ministers is that they prefer to read the lesson they are preaching from immediately before the sermon, so that it is fresh in people's minds. Very strange!

Another hymn would then follow the Gospel and, thereafter, prayers of thanksgiving and intercession were offered. This gave rise to the main liturgical criticism of the 'Hymn Sandwich'. The place for such prayers in a non-sacramental service is after the sermon. This 'dry-mass' (as William Maxwell affectionately called it) should, by strongly accentuating thanksgiving and concern for others, arise as a direct response to the preaching of the Word of God and also prepare the people for the eventual fuller expression of such gratitude within a regular eucharistic context. It is encouraging to find that more and more of our congregations now place these prayers after the sermon, though that does not necessarily mean they are prepared to take the final step to the Lord's Table!

But in the traditional 'hymn-sandwich', after the Gospel had been read followed by the prayers, a hymn was usually sung, the nature of which was determined more by personal preference rather than on any liturgical grounds. This 'loose canon' of a hymn was often followed by an interlude (*sic*) of sorts. We have never really known how to deal with the church notices that have to be made (or do they?), but this was the place where they were slotted in, although today they are usually presented at the very beginning of the service. They concluded with an invitation to make the offering (frequently mis-named the 'collection' or 'offertory') for the work of the church. This 'interlude', admittedly, did have some practical advantages. It was rather like the interval after the seventh inning in an American baseball game (called the 'Seventh Inning Stretch'). It is a chance to take a breather, look around and perhaps have a little chat with your neighbour!

It provided a break before the 'high spot' – the preaching of the Word. The offering was then dedicated, followed by a doxology or a hymn or both. This latter was invariably a hymn of the Holy Spirit, an invocation that the Word of God would be proclaimed through the words of the preacher and that those who waited upon that Word, (including the minister), would be nourished and challenged.

In an earlier time the sermons were never less than twenty minutes, and some a good deal longer. But after they were delivered things came to a rapid conclusion, as they still do in many churches today, with a final hymn in keeping with, one would hope, what had just been preached. The service concluded with the benediction.

At its best, there was, and is, shape and content to such worship and it does not deserve to be dismissed patronisingly as a 'Hymn Sandwich'. When those people, cited in chapter 3, thanked me for conducting an 'old-fashioned' service, what they were probably trying to say was that it was good to be at a service which had shape, one which felt 'right', and which the inclusion of five carefully selected hymns had helped to enhance.

All worship needs to be embodied in form and, as William Maxwell has stressed, to suppose that the choice lies between form and no form is to imagine a false antithesis: 'Form there must always be …. to eliminate form from worship, all words and acts would require to be eliminated.' [2] Even in the most informal acts of worship which their proponents praise for their seeming 'spontaneity', form is never altogether absent. Wherever there are prayers (even extempore ones), announcements, songs, testimonies, sermons, an offering and the like, worship cannot claim simply to be spontaneous through and through. Charismatics have to be careful when they criticize liturgy on the grounds that there is a sameness about it, a sameness which they are bold to suggest stifles the free movement of the Holy Spirit. It is a criticism that could well back-fire.

---

2   Maxwell: op.cit. p40

Maxwell, however, goes on to warn against formal worship, which is not the same thing, and which can all too often be an empty shell. All worship is open to this criticism, whether it be of the 'hymn sandwich' variety or a High Mass or even a Quaker Meeting. Nonetheless, we have to be wary of belittling services which we are quick to judge to be formless. There is often more going on than meets the immediate eye and, in this regard, the Reformed 'dry-mass', with its prominent place for hymnody, was, and is, no exception.

To dismiss it summarily is to forget how effective hymnody can be in enhancing the act of worship, in deepening faith, and in renewing commitment. Hymns have also acted as credal statements in many churches where the Creed is not normally a part of the service. The Hymn Book has played, for many of us, a similar role to that which the Prayer Book has played for the Anglican Church. We only need to call to mind the hymns of John and Charles Wesley, with their influence on the Methodist tradition and beyond, and Isaac Watts, to whom religion was a 'duty and delight'. But hymn-writing was by no means the province of 'dissenters' alone, especially after the appearance of the Church of England hymn book '*Ancient and Modern*' in 1861. The latter finalised the process of converting the Church of England to hymn-singing and had a lasting effect on its worship as well, even though the Book of Common Prayer makes no provision for the singing of hymns. En passant, it is interesting to note that the Orthodox Churches have no concept of hymnody as congregational singing.

Ian Bradley, writing in the *Tablet* for December 25th, 1999, in an article in which *Tablet* book reviewers were asked to nominate their own most important books of the previous hundred years, wrote: 'The accolade of greatest influence on my life I think must go to the 1933 edition of the *English Hymnal*, the hymn collection first put together in 1906 by Percy Dearmer and Ralph Vaughan Williams. It has influenced my faith and coloured my Christian pilgrimage by filling it with companions, images and phrases from the great treasury of English language hymnody. Hymnbooks are ideal for butterflies like me because each page brings a different subject, a new set of verses and a new tune!' [3]

---

3   The Tablet, 25th December 1999

None of us really appreciate how much our faith owes to the hymns we have sung down the years, even to those hymns whose meaning we did not, at the time, fully grasp, (and perhaps still don't!). They consist of both praise and prayer, but also expose us to teaching and the scriptures, not to mention poetry and music. George Herbert wrote:

'A verse may find him, who a sermon flies,
And turn delight into a sacrifice.' 4

Horace Allen, in a sermon preached in the Marsh Chapel at Boston University, said: 'As a child, this ageing liturgist, regularly on the Lord's Day morning, would raise the hazardous question with his parents, "Do we have to go to Sunday School/Church today?" knowing full well that, short of illness or domestic emergency, there actually was no question. And on the last occasion when we three worshipped together of a Christmas Eve, at the singing of the opening hymn, "O come, all ye faithful", the faith consciousness struck with astonishing force: "No wonder I love this hymn: I've been singing it between these two people for well over fifty years".'

I, too, owe a great debt to the 'hymn-sandwiches' of my youth, and of later years, and nothing said here is meant to down-grade the role of hymns in worship. In the 'shaping-up' of liturgy advocated in these pages, one where preached Word and celebrated Sacrament go hand in hand, the hymn still has an important place.

---

4   The Temple: The Church Porch, i.

Chapter Ten

Shaping up

Shaping Up

In the early 1970s I attended the wedding of two friends of mine in a Roman Catholic Church in London. This was the first Roman Catholic service of any kind at which I had been present since Vatican II and its immediate aftermath. It was a time when the decisions of that Council were still percolating down to the man and woman in the pew. I was intrigued to see that the priest was facing the congregation from behind the altar-table, as had always been the tradition in my own church. Its positioning away from the customary high altar had already been a topic of conversation between my neighbour and myself before the service began. He told me that he was a lapsed catholic and it was obvious that he was also a rather puzzled one. I explained to him that what he saw was one of the outcomes of the deliberations of Vatican II, the latter requiring a foot-note in itself.

Half-way through the service, just when I was musing on how similar the service now was to that in my own church, the celebrant invited us to greet each other with the sign of peace. I turned to my friendly neighbour, thrust out my hand and said 'Peace be with you'. 'Good Lord', he replied, looking at his watch: 'Is it over already? Are you coming to the reception?' It took me a few moments to convince him that the service was by no means over; thereafter, his face registered increasing bewilderment. But he was representative of many of his fellow Roman Catholics in that decade and, it must be said, of a good number since.

In the 20th century, and into the present one, the liturgical and ecumenical movements have often accompanied and complemented each other, and there can be no denying the progress that has been made on both fronts. But the growing consensus at the 'top' between liturgical scholars and ecumenical leaders is taking time to percolate down to the grass-roots at the ordinary congregation's level. Changes to customary ways in worship can be difficult to accept, whether we are Roman Catholics or Protestants.

The giving of the Peace continues to be a prime example of this. One Sunday, at a time when Anglicans were only gradually getting used to it, the student body in a well-known theological college in the UK were sharing the Peace at the Eucharist. A young woman, seeing the vice-principal standing in a state of grand isolation, held out her hands and said: 'Peace be with you'. He replied: 'No thank you; I don't indulge.'!

The main change advocated in these pages is for the return in Reformed churches to a weekly conjoining of the preaching of the Word with the celebration of the Sacrament. It is something on which many Reformed liturgists agree but it can be quite another matter when it comes to congregational reception of the same; many still do not want to 'indulge'.

It should not be assumed, however, that the theologians and liturgists always get it right. Bishop Stephen Sykes warns: 'We have to take seriously, it seems to me, the possibility of a tyrannous use of intellectual power; and there has to be a place in the remarkable system of checks and balances in the living religious tradition where theology is simply not in charge. In the end .... the Christian community at worship is such a place, and .... . here there are grounds for religious knowledge which limit the control which the theologian is tempted to exercise by means of his or her superior articulacy.' [1] In other words, we ignore at our peril the common-sense approach to worship (and to the faith for that matter) which men and women often possess and to which serious attention must always be paid – not least by the one who presides as he or she tries to reflect the scholarly thinking about innovations in worship at the grass roots level. But change there has to be, and this is where the skills of a liturgist have to be finely honed with a pastoral competence.

We have seen that the sometimes berated 'hymn-sandwich' often had a shape and order about it which its detractors chose to ignore, and any down-grading of the hymn as an integral part of worship is not negotiable. This, however, does not imply that the communion should simply be 'tagged on', as it were, to such a format. This did happen even in some of those churches which only 'celebrated'

---

1   Stephen Sykes: The Identity of Christianity; London, SPCK, 1984, p7.

the sacrament two or four times a year. In one of my father's churches it was quite usual to provide an 'interval' after the sermon, which allowed almost half the congregation to 'escape'. Needless to say, he opposed this practice but to little avail.

There was a natural progression where the readings were concerned –Hebrew Scriptures–Psalm–Epistle–Gospel sequence. It is a matter of history that the Gospel has generally followed all other readings, by reason of a certain hierarchical sense of deference and respect as is sometimes signified in some traditions by the posture of standing for the reading of that lesson. There is, however, a deeper meaning in such symbolic arrangements. This has to do with the assumption on the part of all these lectionary systems (see chapter 13) that they are meant to be used at Holy Communion, not primarily at self-contained liturgies of the Word. The conjunction of the aforementioned Lord's Day, Lord's Word and Lord's Supper sequence (chapter 6) is at the heart of the matter. Thus the liturgy moves from the 'West Door' gathering as people come into church (the only appropriate place for 'good-mornings' to be exchanged) to lectern and pulpit and then to the table. It is the word of the gospel lessons which seem to be 'closest' to the sacramental presence and action of the Lord. Thus it is the Lord's own words which lead us through preaching, profession of faith and prayer into the Supper.

It should also be noted that it is not the sermon alone which can expound the biblical texts for the day. The 'Constitution on the Sacred Liturgy' restored to the Roman Catholic Mass the so-called 'Prayers of the Faithful' (para 53) which we in the Reformed tradition would speak of as the 'intercessions' or 'pastoral prayer' or even, as in parts of the USA, the 'concerns of the church'. An official commentary on the Roman Missal says: 'Lastly, stress must be laid on the prayers of the faithful, by which the congregation in a sense make their response to the word of God expounded to them and accepted by them. To make the prayers more effective, care must be taken that they be relevant to the particular assembly.'

Both a credal statement and the intercessory prayers should follow the sermon. This raises several questions, such as: Who writes the texts of these creeds or professions of faith? Who determines the concerns of the prayers and how are they said? Just as we assume the preacher will pray *before* the sermon, what would it mean if just as importantly it is assumed that the people will pray *after* the sermon? Just as the sermon should not be the climax of the whole service but the end-process of the proclamation of the Word set forth in the three readings from Old Testament, Epistle and Gospel, so it should also be viewed as the natural precursor of the communion itself – the proclaimed Word of promise moving smoothly and convincingly into the acted Word, which seals the promise, as two closely bound components in perfect balance. Within such a framework there is ample room for flexibility if such is required. Under skilful presidency the worship need not be thrown off course, even if a chorus is sung here or a banner hung there, or if children gather at the minister's feet for five minutes of chaos (see chapter 15,) or the adults laugh at one of his jokes (or refuse to do so, as the case may well be!). Form, we need to be reminded again, does not necessitate formalism but is the custodian of doctrine and good taste, the guarantor of decency and order, not as ends in themselves but as means to a more perfect praise and, through such, a deepening of faith and commitment: *lex orandi, lex credendi.*

What follows takes for granted Calvin's desire for weekly Word/Sacrament held in tandem with each other, that unity which his successors chose not to follow. The grass-roots level of the church has, indeed some catching up to do here, but it is the conjoining of Word and Sacrament which is increasingly emphasized today in the service books of Reformed churches (See, for example, *The Book of Common Order* of the Church of Scotland[2], *Worship: From the United Reformed Church*[3], and *The Book of Common Worship* of the Presbyterian Church, USA, and the Cumberland Presbyterian Church[4].)

In addition, this revision and composition of Reformed liturgies has its counterpart throughout Roman Catholic and the rest of Protestant Christianity, resulting in an almost universal acceptance of the same service structure. One only needs to look at the contents of the mass and service books of these churches to realize how true this is.

---

2   Edinburgh, The Saint Andrew Press, 1994.
3   London, The United Reformed Church, 2003.
4   Louisville, Kentucky, Westminster/John Knox Press, 1993.

'The amount of cross-fertilization that has taken place between the Churches has blurred the differences between their rites. We find a distinct Liturgy of the Word and Liturgy of the Sacrament. The first has an entrance rite, Old Testament, New Testament and Gospel lections, sermon and intercessions. The second contains the placing of the elements on the table, the eucharistic prayer, usually a fraction [breaking of the bread], the act of communion, and a short post-communion rite with blessing and dismissal. In one sense, to have read one new rite is to have read them all. There is indeed a remarkable consensus.' [5]

The above may be self-explanatory except for the reference to the eucharistic prayer. This is an area where many of our Reformed churches are still at their weakest liturgically, and it requires some comment. This 'great prayer' is central to what is taking place not only at the table but throughout all the action. 'It is to this central or "great" prayer that one looks for a statement, in doxological form, of the meaning which the worshippers intend in the rite as a whole.' [6]

Professor Wainwright is saying that, through this prayer, we enter into the complete narrative at the heart of our faith (more effectively than the sermon simply by itself can do) which renews our sense of identity as the people of God for today. As we have seen, more is involved than a simple remembrance and recitation of the events in the Upper Room. Thus it should include praise for the redemptive history of Israel, which is all too often omitted. 'Bereft of the Israelite identity, "Jesus" becomes a mere unidentified numen whom we will make the servant of whatever self-invented religion we find momentarily convenient. If the church ceases to remember the stories of Abraham and Exodus and the prophets, the isolated remembrance of the one Israelite must soon shrivel.' [7]

Another concern which should be 'remembered' in this prayer, but again is all too often omitted, is how we as Christians relate to creation. There should be a cosmic character about the liturgy. 'The communion should be seen as an action uniting heaven and earth, embracing and permeating all creation. The Son of God

---

5   John Fenwick and Bryan Spinks: Worship in Transition – the Twentieth Century Liturgical Movement. Edinburgh, T&T Clark, 1995.

6   Geoffrey Wainwright: Doxology; London, Epworth Press, 1980, p296.

7   Robert W Jenson: Visible Words – The Interpretation and Practice of Christian Sacraments; Minneapolis, USA, Fortress Press, 1978, p96.

became man in order to restore all creation, in one supreme act of praise, to the One who made it from nothing. He, the Eternal High Priest who by the blood of the Cross entered the eternal sanctuary, thus gives back to the Creator and Father all creation redeemed.' [8]

Finally the eucharistic prayer in its eschatological emphasis reminds us that we are being fed for the rest of the journey until God's kingdom is seen to be overall, thus bringing the offering of our thanks and praise to a fitting climax before the act of communion itself. It is sad, however that what passes for a eucharistic prayer in much reformed worship today is of a truncated nature. It is often limited to the events of the Last Supper and, as such, has been partly responsible for perpetuating an over-penitential emphasis at the Lord's Table.

On a more pragmatic level, recovery of the place of the eucharistic prayer also provides the best opportunity for a fuller participation on the part of all the people. (See also the following chapter). Tad Guzie of the University of Calgary writes: 'We are still in the grip of a eucharistic theology that focuses on the elements of bread and wine, rather than on the act of giving thanks (i.e. "eucharist-ing") by breaking bread and sharing a cup. Liturgically, we are still insecure about *enacting* a table liturgy that speaks loud and clear: we are afraid of setting the table, proclaiming the great prayer of thanksgiving, breaking bread and sharing the bread and wine in a way that would vividly involve the entire community. Isn't it the case that in most parishes, respect for the consecrated elements takes precedence over the community's act of thanksgiving and sharing?' [9]

We might be surprised to learn that this 'respect for the consecrated elements' is something that take precedence in many of our Reformed churches just as it has done in Roman Catholic churches, but there is some truth in this. The habit of holding a morsel of bread, and then a thimbleful of wine in the hand, until everybody has been served, and only then eating and drinking together, (not exactly how we conduct ourselves at the ordinary meal table – that is, by taking synchronised mouthfuls!), is not only aesthetically displeasing in its execution, being more reminiscent of a toast to a departed loved one, but it gives unnecessary

---

8   Ecclesia de Eucharistia – Encyclical letter of Pope John Paul II
9   Tad Guzie: Landscape of Praise: op.cit. p188.

prominence to the elements as we clutch and stare at them until everybody has been served. It is the action as a whole which is important, that movement which should begin at the 'Great Entrance'. (The carrying in of the Bible at the beginning of the service is the 'Little Entrance', and marks the first movement in the service where the breaking of the Word is paramount.)

The history of the Great Entrance goes back long before the Reformation, to the time when the laity brought their gifts of bread and wine with them to the assembly, which were then presented at the altar by the deacons. Dom Gregory Dix has pointed out how, from the fourth century onwards, East and West differed considerably on this. Interestingly, the Reformed Church has tended to show more affinity with the Eastern practice.

'In the East in later times it was the custom for the laity to bring their oblations to the sacristy or to a special table in the church before the service began .... The deacons fetched them from there when they were wanted at the offertory (the beginning of the eucharist proper). This little ceremony soon developed into one of the chief points of "ritual splendour" in the Syrian-Byzantine rites, and became the "Great Entrance".' [10] En passant, and as Brian Gerrish has pointed out, Dix's sad travesty of Calvin's doctrine of the Lord's Supper[11] rests on the assumption that Protestantism means individualism. Dix is also regarded as being somewhat out of date today, even by some Anglicans.

'Ritual splendour' is perhaps not the first description that comes to mind where the Great Entrance in the Reformed tradition is concerned but, at its best, it provides a moment of impressive dignity and quiet spectacle when, with the offering of money together with the elements (a combination which is called the 'offertory' as distinct from the 'offering' but, as already mentioned in chapter 9, the two are often being confused), a hymn of praise is sung and the procession enters the church. It is not so common as formerly, in part because of smaller congregations but also because of the propensity to dismiss it in some circles as pretentious (*sic*).

---

10   Dom Gregory Dix: The Shape of the Liturgy; London, Adam and Charles Black, 1945, p120.
11   Ibid., 632-633.

This is sad. The alternative, as often occurs, is to have the elements placed upon the table from the very beginning of the service, sometimes covered with a cloth. At the appropriate moment, they are then 'unveiled' with great solemnity. But this can give the wrong signals, not least by drawing once again too much attention to the elements. It has an affinity with certain Roman Catholic practices with which we, as Reformed church people, should not be too comfortable. Gregory Dix, writing about the difference between the Eastern and Western Church, contrasts the Great Entrance in the East and the theology behind it with 'the mere laying of a host upon the paten by the Western sacristan without prayer or ceremony of any sort whatever – just so that it will be there when the priest uncovers the vessels. We find on the one hand the gorgeous Eastern "Great Entrance".... and on the other the pouring of a little wine into the chalice by the Western priest at the altar with a muttered prayer while the choir sing a snippet of a psalm and the people sit.' [12]

Dix, of course, was writing well before Vatican II and Rome has certainly 'caught up' to an extent, whereas many Protestants have not. The table, already laid, and the unveiling of the same have more in common with former Catholic and pre-Vatican II practices than with the intention of traditional Reformed understanding.

The Great Entrance begins that part of the service which is dominated by the eucharistic prayer and has an integral place in relationship to it. But this prayer also contextualises other words and actions: the Sursum Corda ('Lift up your hearts'); the saying or singing of the Sanctus ('Holy, holy, holy'); the Peace; the Agnus Dei ('Lamb of God'); the Words of Institution and the Lord's Prayer. At the heart of all this should be the 'Epiclesis', that is the invocation of the Holy Spirit without whom there is no 'real presence'. Apart from the narrative significance of the above actions embraced within the eucharistic prayer, under skilful presidency it can provide opportunity for a fuller participation on the part of the congregation. It is encouraging to see this happening in some of our churches.

An even more serious matter is the omission of the Epiclesis altogether. This should concern us if for no other reason than it was the Calvinist tradition, above all others, that stressed the importance of the invocation of the Spirit. (Wesley's

---

12   Ibid p121

hymns on the Lord's Supper also did this.) Calvin's stress on 'efficacious memorial', not just of the past but, of the present and future, was closely dependent on his doctrine of the leading of the Spirit in these matters. No service was complete without the invocation of the same, but many is the time I have listened for it in Reformed churches and felt peculiarly disturbed when it was absent. It does seem odd that some ministers, who rightly invoke the Spirit at the beginning of their sermons, fail to do likewise at the commencement of the sacrament!

An Anglican, Canon A M Allchin, reminds us of Calvin's emphasis in this matter: 'In the Eucharist we do not remember a Master long-since dead and absent. We recall one who in the act of recalling becomes present with us. Here above all is the effective presence of the past in the present .... It is agreed that all this happens in the power and energy of the Holy Spirit. The belief that in the Eucharist the Spirit is active,that the Sacrament is in some sense the constant presence of Pentecost in the Church, as well as the constant presence of Christ's death and resurrection, has always had a central place in the theology of the Christian East. In the West amongst Catholics and many Protestants it has not been so much rejected as forgotten – *John Calvin is an honourable exception here* (my italics), and so are the Scottish divines who stand in succession to the doctors of Aberdeen. Suddenly this element of belief has become powerful again amongst Catholics and Protestants alike. It has proved to be a help on the way to resolving old controversies and to discovering new meanings .... Here are modest signs of the growing power of the Spirit in the Church.'[13] This is encouraging, and things have moved on somewhat since Canon Allchin wrote those words. But those of us who have 'moved on' must be careful lest we fall into the pharisaical habit of labelling services which may omit formulae such as the epiclesis as 'invalid'. The Spirit of God is quite capable of getting through in spite of our liturgical lapses. But before we can even begin to think of moving from a quarterly or a monthly celebration, we must ensure that our present services are in as good a shape as possible. This means that simply to have a weekly celebration in the same way as we do now would be counter-productive.

---

13   A M Allchin: The Dynamic of Tradition; London, Darton, Longman and Todd, 1981, pp123-124.

'To replicate the Lord's Supper on a weekly basis just as it is now celebrated monthly would be to court disaster. Until we develop genuine concern about the quality of celebration, greater frequency will reform little. Pastors need special sensitivity about the sign value of every aspect of the rites, not as a fussy rubrical matter, but as genuine pastoral concern that people better perceive and express what is ultimately real for them.' [14] At the end of the service it is fitting that the vessels are carried out in procession in a similar way to that in which they were brought in. As to the disposal of any remaining bread and wine, Professor Jenson must have the last word: 'Protestants who ceremonialize an act of transformation, and then blithely put the remaining elements back in box and bottle, speak a visible word of unbelief in the sacramental presence.'! [15]

One other matter, by way of parenthesis to all of the above, must be mentioned. Although there now exists a remarkable consensus concerning the words and actions at communion, it is a different matter when it comes to the theology that lies behind them. The question, for instance, of 'the moment of consecration' is a prime example. It is an important question if you have a doctrine of the Real Presence which teaches that the bread and wine are actually turned into the Body and Blood of Christ when the appropriate invocation is pronounced; it is not so important when your firm belief in the real presence arises out of the actions in the service as a whole. Different traditions have their own particular emphases at this point where the preparation of bread and wine is concerned and on the significance of the actions associated with this, but none should allow us to treat the elements in a casual manner.

The use of identical words by different traditions masks these matters, but this should not disturb us too much. It is perhaps a necessary stage on the way which leads to a greater all-round understanding, and to the enriching of our experience by learning from each other.

What, however, if the whole service of word and sacrament is to be filled out in the ways suggested, is the place for participation in the liturgy by the whole people of God.

---

14   James White, The Christian Century January 27, 1982.
15   Jenson, op.cit. p112.

Chapter Eleven

Participation

Participation

In 1962 I was approached by the Head of Religious Broadcasting at the BBC enquiring if I would be willing to conduct a series of three services from my church to be screened on national television on consecutive Sunday mornings. It was an offer which a young minister could not refuse, not least because there was only the BBC at that time and, so, this really meant national coverage. An ego-trip was, of course, involved but that need not detain us here.

My excitement was shared by the congregation. After all, to be on the 'telly' in those days was a sure-fire way to be the envy of one's friends. There was great enthusiasm and growing excitement as the first of the Sundays approached and there would surely be no need to send out a three-line whip, as often has to be the case today when a local church service is broadcast. Our church was full every Sunday and there would be no problem in this respect – or so I thought. Confidence was such that extra chairs were brought in from the local community centre and placed in the aisles in order to seat all the non-regulars who, it was assumed, would also wish to be 'on the telly'.

I was, however, mortified when on the day itself the church was less than half-full. The imported chairs had to be hidden away and those sitting in the side aisles were ushered into the centre, so at least enabling camera angles to give the impression of a full house. I was also furious and, immediately after the broadcast, rushed out into the parish like a wild thing and proceeded to knock on the doors of the 'regulars' demanding why, on this unique occasion, they had chosen to absent themselves. I was given almost identical answers: 'But we wanted to see it on the telly'! (These were pre-video days). Word soon spread describing the appearance of the dishevelled and troubled cleric on their door-steps and, not willing to face my wrath again, the final two services presented a much different picture. The community centre chairs were back in place and the cameras were able to rove at will.

Reflecting nowadays on that incident, I am not only amused by it but I can discern another, albeit subconscious, reason why so many stayed away. Yes, overwhelmingly it had to do with seeing the church they attended on the television, but I now believe that quite a number would not have reacted in this way if the service to which they were normally accustomed had involved them more than it did in its regular 'production'. I did, and said, everything in it and never thought for one moment that there was anything deficient in that. Neither did the members, but it meant they had no sense of personal responsibility for it and so could quite easily continue their 'spectator' role, only this time from the comfort of their arm-chairs.

They wanted to see their church on the screen, but in a sense it was not a church for whose worship they felt in any way responsible.

I realise now how much I was beholden to the particular style of worship which was then taken for granted in the training we received in our theological colleges and seminaries, assuming, as they all did, an exclusive role in the sanctuary for the ordained minister. I am happy that it is now almost taken for granted that there should be greater participation in the conduct of public worship. When William Maxwell wrote about the importance of the contribution of the worshippers to a service, he was right in suggesting that services, which took such into account, would then be no longer formal, that they would be vibrant with spirit and would mean more to the members of the congregation. He was certainly ahead of the Church of Scotland of his day, but I suspect he would have some reservations about present developments, as do I.

In recent years there has been a growing tendency to judge an act of worship as 'successful', or otherwise, according to how many people are involved in its presentation. There is much more 'participation' by a cross-section of our congregations than there ever has been before and much of it is to be welcomed. But too many cooks can spoil the liturgical broth!

James White draws a distinction between passive and active participation. He defines passive participation as relating to people who hear or see someone else do something. Watching liturgical dance, for instance, would be a passive activity. On the other hand, he defines active participation as relating to people doing things by themselves, such as praying, singing, preaching and dancing. Both kinds involve different levels of participation. [1] It is a useful distinction but it can be misleading. Listening and looking may seem to be a passive stance, but this is deceptive; they can belie the very opposite. When, for instance, the Word of God is preached, no one, least of all the preacher, can estimate what effect it is having on the worshipers who hear it. Whenever I have listened to sermons, I would not, in most cases, describe my reception of them as passive. Sometimes they have inspired and moved me; occasionally they have made me angry; and less often they have bored me; but to suggest my state has been inactive is misleading.

On the other hand, the presence of several 'active' participants in a service can, paradoxically, have a negative effect on those of us who are not similarly involved or inclined, and be inhibiting; liturgical dance does this to me, and I am not alone (Sigmund Freud, take note!). This, however, is not an argument for the suppression of the latter, and similar happenings, altogether. It is rather a plea for more sensitivity when it comes to incorporating such into the liturgy. One person's 'turn-on' can be several others' 'turn-off'.

One of the most significant statements of recent years concerning the role of the people in worship comes from Vatican II in its recommendation for: 'full, conscious, and active participation'. There are many examples where the Roman Catholic Church today has taken these guidelines to heart and from which the Reformed churches must learn; in fact, as I have already mentioned, while attending some of their liturgies I have felt they are more reformed than we are! Before we proceed, therefore, we need to remind ourselves once again of the nature and purpose of reformed worship; only then can we assess the kind of participation which helps to fulfil its aims.

At its heart, Reformed worship is (or should be) doxological in form. It glorifies and praises God the creator, the sustainer and the renewer of his creatures. It must not be reduced to a means to some other end, such as personal growth, the health of the nation, or the success of the church. These are not bad ends in themselves, but the purpose of the liturgy is first and supremely to worship God.

---

1   James White; Op.Cit, chapter 1

Dr Douglas Ottati, of Union Seminary, Richmond, Virginia, spells out the direction in which reformed worship must go and, in doing so, demonstrates obliquely what authentic participation should be. Stressing that it directs the people of God toward a communion with Him in community with others, he writes: 'This should be clearly understood from the variety of emotional responses and sensibilities that reforming worship may call forth in the worshipper.' [2]

In defence of many of the services of the church of my youth, although often totally in the hands of one man (*sic*), they often succeeded in evoking the 'emotional responses and sensibilities' as mentioned above. It would be disingenuous not to acknowledge this or not to recognise the congregational 'participation' that it involved, albeit of a 'passive' variety. It would be to ignore how often skilled presidency, and not least the preaching ability of the president, in the hands of an individual who 'did it all', could be very effective in enabling the qualities mentioned by Ottati to be awakened in the hearts and minds of the worshippers. They were far from being passive in their response, one which was often verbalised in their hymn-singing even if nowhere else. What is, however, being suggested is that in today's climate there is a need for these congregational responses to be articulated in more open fashion. This is not to invite a free-for-all; in some services I have attended the impression given is that everyone is trying to get in on the act. This is not what the priesthood of all believers is about, (see chapter 13) and there are dangers in allowing a *laissez-faire* approach to worship to take control.

The logical outcome of encouraging such 'permissiveness' can already be glimpsed in the 'do-it-yourself' weddings and funeral services wherein responsibility is often handed over by some ministers to the main participants (with the exception of the corpse!). One minister tells how a family insisted, against his advice, that they should sing at the crematorium one of their departed dad's favourite songs: 'Smoke gets in your eyes'! Another assures me that, on a similar occasion, but one where the deceased had committed suicide, the family had also asked for his favourite song, namely Frank Sinatra singing: 'I did it my way'!

---

2   Douglas F Ottati: Reforming Protestantism; Louisville, Kentucky, Westminster John Knox Press, 1995, pp120-121.

Today, when worship committees or liturgical teams or engaged couples write their own liturgies, it needs to be done carefully and in close consultation with the one who presides at worship.

En passant, a question can be raised concerning the degree of participation that actually exists in smaller groups, such as those held in people's homes. It would be thought that these are the places where the contribution of everyone is paramount, and, therefore, they are good 'training grounds' for a more public involvement on a Sunday. This can certainly be the case, but it is interesting to note that even at this modest level, within what would seem to be a very democratic setting, there is often one person to whom everyone looks for guidance. The basis of membership may well be personal experience recognised and authenticated by the group, but confirmed by the group leader. Others can come to the meeting but, unless they also experience the call of the Spirit, they do not have a full role to play, can even feel excluded. No special education is expected of the members or the leaders. Marks of power include a familiarity with biblical quotations, experience and external signs.

Of course it is good that, on a Sunday, the presiding minister's voice is, in the majority of cases today, not the only one that is heard in our services; but he or she must take more responsibility, wherever possible, for the voices that are heard. If we think nothing of having a weekly choir practice guided by the organist and/or choir leader, and do so in order that their contribution will be as good as possible, why, for instance, is there not a similar rehearsal for those who are appointed to read the Sunday lessons and pray the prayers? Since my retirement I have listened to many readers in several countries in churches of different traditions; only very occasionally has it been done well. The most irritating aspect of it is that so often three lessons are read from three different translations from the Bible, for no other reason than the individual preferences of the readers. I have heard ministers preach from texts which, although from the set readings, are from another translation from the one read. This is sheer sloppiness, as is the reluctance to put the readers through their paces so that matters of diction, and their own understanding of the context of the passage in question, may be improved.

Another irritant is the failure to familiarise active participants with microphone technique. It is good that many of our churches now have this facility, and doubly welcome that it is often accompanied by the loop system for the hard of hearing. But far too many readers assume that the existence of the microphone frees them from any need to project their voices, albeit in a slightly different way than if there were no microphone. Too close a proximity can give rise to 'popping' when the letter 'p' is pronounced (which it frequently is!); too great a distance from it and the microphone might as well not be there. All these 'little' details, if not attended to, can annoy and sometimes ruin a service for others. If we are at all serious about the priority of weekly worship, and our participation in it, it should not be too much to expect people to meet on a weekly basis with the minister to study the set lectionary readings; to learn from him/her what the text is – maybe even suggest what the text ought to be and discuss the sermon's possible content; and be put through their paces in rehearsal. If this is simply not practical, then the very least that should be required would be for those concerned to meet for a brief time after morning service on the previous Sunday. (As this begs the question concerning the role of the minister, see chapters 13 and 14).

I like the growing custom of the intercessory prayers being said by a member of the congregation, but the same principles also apply here. The content of these prayers must bear some relation to what was said in the sermon. Above all, the person leading the prayer has to be reminded that he or she must allow their personal feelings and concerns to be swallowed up and permit the prayer to be prayed through them rather than by them. The failure to do this has often spoiled my 'passive' participation in a service, and I am sure that, along with other leaders of prayer, I, too, have been guilty of allowing personal feelings to intrude over much. Professor James White, a former Moderator of the General Assembly of the Church of Scotland, (and not to be confused with the James White already quoted in these pages), in a lecture entitled 'Discerning the Spirit in Worship', said: 'I find the attempts of enthusiastic young ministers to think up new sins to confess on my behalf on a Sunday morning, usually results in my playing a kind of game with them. "Missed me that time" I say. Sometimes one wonders if the minister is unloading his own sense of guilt on the congregation .... . A friend of mine told how he almost disgraced himself in church one Sunday morning because when he was raising his head after one of those very hearty prayers of confession, his wife leant over to him and whispered, "He's been tying his wife to the bed-post again."! [3]

---

3   Lecture delivered at Westminster College, (The United Reformed Church), Cambridge.

Another irritant is the failure of so many of our congregations to respond with the 'Amen', a response which is their obligation. It means 'Yes, truly', and acknowledges that they have agreed with the sentiments expressed and identified with them. The presider at worship has to be aware that even this calls for 'rehearsal', albeit within the act of worship itself.

None of the above is to suggest ideas that were not known to, and promulgated by, the original Reformers. There were preachers' workshops, begun in Zurich in 1525. The preachers of the day gathered in the cathedral five days a week for their school. A selected passage was examined in Latin and Hebrew or Greek. Then its use in a sermon was discussed and finally a sermon preached on it.

A similar practice was followed once a week in Lasco's Church of the Strangers in London, and in the English refugee congregation in Geneva. Here all members of the congregation were encouraged to present questions to the ministers through a committee. Many other examples could be given of such 'participation' to demonstrate that what is being suggested here is not something radically new, but an attempt to recover what had been formerly encouraged but then fell into disuse.

That the Reformers were more in favour of congregational participation than we sometimes have given them credit for can be seen in their attitude to the psalms, especially metrical versions of the psalms. Erasmus had pointed them in this direction: 'They chant nowadays in our churches in what is an unknown tongue and nothing else .... let them sing the psalms like rational beings ....' [4]

This aspect of worship was aided by Calvin's unexpected attitude to music, as stated in his prefaces to be 1542 and 1545 editions of the metrical psalter: 'It has power to enter the heart like wine poured into a vessel, with good or evil effect'. In worship, in particular, it 'has great force and vigour to move and inflame the hearts of men to invoke and praise God with a more vehement and ardent zeal'. Hastings Nichols, on whom I have drawn for the above information, writes: 'Metrical psalmody swept Europe as the most characteristic mark and powerful attraction of Reformed worship. Even strict Lutherans spoke with some envy and irritation of "la sirène calviniste".' [5]

---

4   J A Froude: Life and Letters of Erasmus; Charles Scribner's Sons, 1894, pp122ff.
5   Ibid., p36.

To know and love the psalms was the mark of a Reformer and there are some signs that their rediscovery as central to participatory worship on the part of the congregation as a whole is beginning gradually to take place, especially with the growing use of responsive antiphons. It is important that the pace should quicken. The psalms, after all, have played a crucial role in the faith experience of God's people through the centuries and on the ecumenical scene today there is an exciting cross-fertilisation taking place which exposes us of the Reformed tradition to settings in addition to the familiar metrical ones, as the hymn book of the United Reformed Church demonstrates. [6]

This cross-fertilisation is also taking place where many hymns are concerned so that, all in all, Christians have a better chance than ever before to sing from the same hymn sheet. In addition, all this is a restoration that can help to remind the people of God of their participatory role in worship, and on that count alone is deserving of encouragement.

But how can we really get our Sunday act together? Many questions are raised by all that has gone before, and I must now try to go some way towards answering at least one or two of them.

---

6   'Rejoice and Sing': Oxford University Press, 1991.

Chapter Twelve

High Drama

preferred to serve the people seated at long tables in the nave. And the Zwinglians and Anglicans served the people in their places (*sic*). In the forms of ceremonial in which it was necessary for the communicants to pass the bread and cup to each other there was usually conscious reference to the communion of saints. As Calvin had put it, 'It is as if one said that the saints are gathered into the society of Christ on the principle that whatever benefits God confers upon them, they should in turn share with one another'. [1] He adds that Calvin refused to make an issue of whether the bread and cup were to go from hand to hand, or to be served to each individually by a minister or elder, or whether the wine be white or red (it never apparently occurred to him that it might be unfermented!) or the bread leavened or unleavened: 'Such matters were indifferent and left to the discretion of the church' [2].

I am with Calvin in all this and I would hope that the above has reminded us that there is a legitimate place for a variety of practices. If the 'problem' of the length of service seems to remain unanswered, it may be because one of the above alternatives has not yet been tried. I discovered this in the United States, by attending a Roman Catholic mass in a packed church. Apart from the main altar, there were several other altars around the building, and they served the communicants who had been skilfully directed to their space and who partook standing around the table. Several hundred received within fifteen minutes, and in a dignified way. It also lent itself better to the involvement of all the children (see chapter 15) in a way in which serving in the pews does not.

In the final resort, however, much depends upon the skill of the one who presides at the sacrament. The best presidents have a sense of theatre; after all, it is a drama which is being re-enacted and, like all real drama, it needs direction and choreographing. The very word 'theatre' comes from the Greek 'theatron' which means 'the place of viewing'. In some churches, like St Paul's in London, the chancel is still referred to on occasions as 'the theatre'.

It is appropriate that the one who presides should usually be the preacher as well. It is fitting that the one who has broken the Word in the pulpit should also break the Bread of Life at the table. The one who presides should have an overall

---

1   Nichols: op.cit. pp49-50.
2   Ibid., p50.

role, one akin to that of Master of Ceremonies (in fact, in some traditions that is what he is called) and, like all good MCs, he/she should assume a watchful eye over proceedings which, one would hope, have already been rehearsed beforehand. (This is even more essential when the sacrament is not celebrated on a weekly basis. A minister friend, who presides at communion only once a quarter, told me that even long-serving elders tended to look like frightened rabbits caught in the headlights of a car as they tried to remember what to do next!). I also believe that, as an ordained minister of the Church Catholic, the minister's presence symbolises, actualises, the catholicity of the sacrament; but this is to beg a question dealt with more fully in chapter 13.

In 'Encounter with God'[3] the authors stress what we have already noted, that almost all new eucharistic liturgies have virtually the same structure. They acknowledge that, while there is some variety as to the sequence and emphasis, fundamentally it is an integrated whole. Here is an order of service which they have slightly adapted from 'Baptism, Eucharist and Ministry'[4] and which is quite compatible with what has been outlined in the last two chapters, give or take one or two minor matters. I have also made one or two additions of my own. If it does look daunting (and hymns are largely omitted) in its length, remember that eight of the 'items' are all included within the one Eucharistic Prayer.

> Little Entrance (The Bible)
> Hymn of Praise
> Prayers: Adoration, Confession and the Gospel word of Pardon.
> Proclamation of the Word of God (scripture and sermon)
> Confession of faith
> Intercessions for the Church and the World
> Offertory
> The Great Entrance

> ----------

---

3   Forrester, McDonald, and Tellini: Edinburgh, T&T Clark, 1996.
4   Baptism, Eucharist and Ministry (Faith and Order paper 111); Geneva, World Council of Churches, 1982, pp15-16.

Eucharistic Prayer:
>   Thanksgiving to the Father for the marvels of creation, redemption
>   and sanctification:
>   the words of Christ's Institution of the sacrament:
>   the anamnesis or memorial of the great acts of redemption, passion,
>   death, resurrection, ascension and Pentecost:
>   the epiclesis (i.e. the invocation of the Holy Spirit on the community and
>   the elements of bread and wine):
>   consecration of the faithful to God:
>   reference to the communion of saints:
>   prayer for the return of the Lord and the definitive manifestation of
>   his kingdom:
>   The Lord's Prayer

Sign of reconciliation and peace (though there is some differences between
traditions in the positioning of the latter):
eating and drinking in communion with Christ and with each member of
the Church:
Post-communion prayer and collect:
Dismissal and Blessing.

Reading the above will do nothing to allay the fears of those who are adamant that such would take up an inordinate length of time to complete. It need not, and I challenge them at least to try and, I hope, be pleasantly surprised! (I have experienced services of a more extempore format which have taken far longer).

The above, however, is all very well, but the situation in at least England and Wales (there are still exceptions in parts of Scotland, Northern Ireland and the USA) is such that the smaller congregation tends to be the norm and the larger ones are few and far between. One 'solution' could be for a group of reformed churches to come together once a month in the most convenient building and to engage in such a liturgy. After all, in a former day, Methodists demonstrated how a Sunday evening gathering together of a group of their congregations in the local Central Hall to hear the Word preached, often to a 'full house,' could be a memorable experience. The same might be the possible result where the Sacrament is concerned. There are, however, particular opportunities where the smaller congregation is concerned and which are worth exploring.

Jesus said: 'Where two or three are gathered in my name, there I am in the midst' (Matthew 18:20). In its context it refers to the power of decision-making within a small group but it can just as legitimately be applied to gatherings for prayer and study as well.

'The eucharist did not begin in large assemblies. It began in everyday Jewish table fellowship. In Luke's Gospel, meals are the setting for much of Jesus' teaching. When Levi the tax collector became a follower of Jesus, he hosted a dinner .... the meal became a healing and reconciling event, and a sign of the meal that Jesus will eat and drink with us in the kingdom (Luke 5).' [5]

Dr Guzie remarks that St Luke's Gospel offers us a 'basic' eucharistic theology that is especially characteristic of small groups gathered in Jesus' name: 'What the breaking of bread conveys in this context is forgiveness, welcome and mutual acceptance, commitment to caring for others and sharing one's blessings. While these themes are not absent from large assemblies, they are bound to be experienced with greater intensity and clarity in small groups.' He adds a word of warning however: 'The intimacy and close union that characterize small groups need to be complemented by the hope and vision of the "great church". Without this vision, micro-churches tend to close in on themselves and focus only on their own concerns." [6]

I can see no reason why the order of service outlined above for the 'macro-church' should not be relevant for the smaller situations. At least many of the 'items' that find a place in the ordering of the former should also be present in the latter. I am thinking especially of the eucharistic prayer. There could even be a small-scale 'Great Entrance' in which, after the proclamation of the Word,

---

5   Tad Guzie; op.cit p188.
6   Tad Guzie; ibid. p189.

(and this kind of setting does facilitate the dialogue/discussion format – especially as all the attenders in many of our churches could sit around the table), two or three go to the vestry and bring in not only the vessels but a white cloth for the table. The visible setting of the table can be a very moving and significant part of the action. The smaller assembly also gives greater scope for the incorporation of silence in the worship and is, possibly, a means of introducing the common cup to those congregations which are not accustomed to it. If any progress is going to be made on the larger scale, a positive beginning could be made at the smaller level. It must not be used as a means to an end, but it certainly could be a fertile field for sowing the seeds of eventual change.

If, however, these important matters are to be pursued, there is one other issue which now has to be faced, and it has been put off long enough. This is the way in which the role of the minister is perceived today. It is an area where there is a considerable difference of opinion within the Reformed churches themselves, but it is also exercising debate at a wider level throughout many other churches as well.

I am convinced that the Reformed churches need to recover a once-held 'high' doctrine of the Ministry of Word and Sacraments, albeit one which goes hand-in-hand with an increasing partnership with the rest of the people of God. But it must not be displaced by the latter.

Chapter Thirteen

Ministry in Question

Ministry in Question

My Scottish mother was a Glasgow girl and lived there until she married my father in 1929. At the time of their engagement she was the guide captain and he was the young assistant minister in the same parish church. I learned a great deal from her concerning the church of her youth, a church which had hardly changed at all by the time I was born. The church I grew up in had more in common with that of my mother and father than with today's church. One fundamental change has been the difference in perception today of the minister's role.

Mother had three brothers and three sisters. One of her vivid memories as a child was of the visits of the local minister to their home. He would have warned my grandmother (my grandfather was killed in the First World War) in advance of his coming and, when the time arrived, all the family would assemble in the rarely used front room, dressed in their Sunday best. The minister was always dressed in frock coat, striped trousers, clerical collar and wore a top hat! After the latter was dispensed with, along with a few polite preliminaries, it was down to serious business. 'Meg' he would say, addressing the eldest first, 'What is the first article of the catechism?' That was relatively easy and my aunt would reply: 'Man's chief end is to glorify God and enjoy him for ever.' But by the time he got round to the eldest it was not so simple, with questions ranging from more obscure parts of the catechism to the commandments and beyond. Although, however, the minister's departure was the occasion for a certain amount of relief, he was, nonetheless, a respected figure, even held in affection.

On Sundays, of course, he was very much the dominant figure, often the only figure, where the conduct of public worship was concerned. If I as a wee boy had mistaken him for God (see chapter 2), those who did not still looked up to him as one set apart for his holy office. Many of these men were highly educated scholars in their own right, though often coming – like my father – from very humble backgrounds. They were usually held in high regard in the wider community, giving the church, in a representative capacity, a high profile.

My father had a 'high' view of the ministry, as did most of his contemporaries. Although a very modest man, he would nevertheless affirm that the minister was *primus inter pares* – first among equals (but definitely first!). Ministers and the ruling elders, as they were significantly called, were subject to the authority of higher courts–the local Presbytery, the area Synod and the General Assembly – but all these were made up of equal male representation from the ranks of ministers and elders and no one else. It was not a democratic system in the modern understanding of that term; it was oligarchic rather than democratic, but it worked. It was the kind of ministry and church government of which, on the whole, Calvin would have approved.

Things are different now in terms of the general perception of the ministry, but conciliar government (rule by councils) still remains (though with greater involvement of women) in, for instance, the Church of Scotland, the Irish Presbyterian Church, the Presbyterian Church (USA), and in the United Reformed Church in the United Kingdom. In the latter denomination the local Church meeting is now considered to be one of such councils, stressing the importance of the role of the whole people of God in the decision-making procedures. The doctrine of the priesthood of all believers is invoked as justification for this and for a lessening of the perception of the role of the minister from that of 'primus' to 'enabler' and 'facilitator' – to use terms often applied today within the areas of education and community development. It is a role that many ministers are content to accept; in the face of declining membership and numbers in the pews, it seems to provide the only alternative to the traditional model. But caution is called for.

Richard Neuhaus talks about the 'inescapable oddity' of the ministerial vocation, the unavoidable 'difference' that the ministry exemplifies. Although he writes with the situation in the United States very much in mind, what he says also could apply to the UK: 'In some seminaries the talk is still about training "enablers", "facilitators", and the like. But what is needed is not the training of religious technicians but the formation of spiritual leaders. It is important for seminaries to impart skills and competencies; it is more important to ignite conviction and the courage to lead. The language of facilitation is cool and low-risk. The language of priesthood and prophecy and the pursuit of holiness is impassioned and perilous.

We cover our fearful choice of the low-risk option with egalitarian talk about the priesthood of all believers. But those who have been touched by the burning coal from the altar, and whose touch has been ratified by the call of the Church, must not pretend that nothing special has happened to them. Such pretence is not humility but blasphemy; it is not modesty but ingratitude; it is not devotion to equality but evasion of responsibility. It is fear, the fear of being different. And when we are afraid to act upon the difference to which we are called, we inhibit others from acting upon the difference to which they are called.' [1]

Neuhaus is right to emphasise that we try to disguise 'our fearful choice of the low-risk option with egalitarian talk of the priesthood of all believers'. When my father, all those years ago, described himself as being '*primus inter pares*', he was not making a value judgment implying he was of superior worth to others and he was certainly not advocating a hierarchical structure of individuals within the church; but neither was he coming down on the side of the egalitarians. He had a special calling to be a minister of Word and Sacraments, and that was an end of the matter!

The doctrine of the priesthood of all believers was formulated to declare that it is through the whole people (the *laos* of God), not through ministers alone, that the ministry of Christ is continued in the world. Ministers are part of the *laos*, 'which has a more all-embracing meaning than the popular connotation of the "laity".' [2]

This Report went on to explain that the doctrine of the priesthood of all believers finds its principal New Testament support in I Peter 2:9 and occasional references in Revelation – 1:6; 5:10. I Peter 2:9 is a notoriously difficult verse to translate and interpret: 'But you are a chosen race, a royal priesthood, a holy nation, God's own people, in order that you may proclaim the mighty acts of him who called you out of darkness into his marvellous light.' But however much it is translated, it is the Church as corporate body which shares in the high priesthood of Christ. The verse is not speaking about the ministry or priesthood of Christians as individuals. 'Priesthood is a corporate description not an individual mandate. It is a function of the community of believers, derived from their participation in the high priesthood of Christ.' [3]

---

1   Neuhaus: op.cit pp210-219.
2   Patterns of Ministry: United Reformed Church, Interim Report 1994, p36.
3   Ibid., p36.

The Report points out that the agenda of the Reformers was to recover that set of relationships between Christ, his people and the ministry, which they perceived to have been lost. Luther, Zwingli and Calvin were not against the ministry but against a particular view of the priestly office.

But a problem that has arisen today, through a mistaken understanding of what the doctrine of the priesthood of all believers is about, lies in the assumption that it is advocating egalitarianism when it comes to church life. Today's society in the West is attracted to the egalitarian ideal, at least as a philosophy, and, as with the non-directive approach to learning and development which has been so prominent in recent years, the Reformed churches have, by a kind of osmosis, tended to follow the secular trend. But any potential embrace of the egalitarian ideal needs to be examined with some care.

The American theologian, the late Paul Lehmann, has written trenchantly on this matter. In the introduction to his last publication, *The Decalogue and a Human Future*, his editor Nancy J Duff explains: 'Lehman rejects the hierarchical structure of relationships among human beings that has been traditionally affirmed by both culture and church .... [but] he also rejects the egalitarian structure which has, since the French Revolution, been proposed in place of hierarchy. Egalitarianism, argues Lehmann, is not substantial enough to break the bonds of hierarchy and establish right relationships among human beings. Its greatest weakness is found in its inability to acknowledge honestly the real differences that exist among human beings, for fear that once these actual differences are acknowledged, differences in value will also be affirmed. In place of both hierarchy and egalitarianism, Lehmann proposes the idea of "reciprocal responsibility", which emphasises the differences among human beings .... without justifying the privileged status of certain groups, as hierarchy does.' [4]

Lehmann himself writes: '.... it has become ominously evident that neither hierarchical nor egalitarian, social, economic, cultural, and political structures are capable of furthering the freedom that being human in this world requires.' [5]

---

4   Paul L Lehmann: The Decalogue and a Human Future; Grand Rapids, Michigan, William B Eerdmans Publishing Co., 1995, p11

5   Ibid., pp 31-32

I believe Lehmann's concept of reciprocal responsibility provides a model for ministry which can best meet the needs of the Reformed churches and provide a fresh understanding of the doctrine of the priesthood of all believers for today. It can do this while, at the same time, upholding Neuhaus's conception of the 'inescapable oddity' of the ministerial vocation. But from where comes the authority for this 'oddity' in the first place?

The understanding of the nature of the ordained ministry has been open to change down the centuries. The New Testament itself provides no one blue-print for it, and the developments and crises of Christian history have brought changes in their wake. The Reformation did not abandon the notion and practice of a special or ordained ministry. Calvin sought to be more scriptural, (though his evidence is not all that strong), with his four-fold pattern of pastor, teacher, elder and deacon. The teacher has disappeared, except in the colleges and as a more informal function; the elder is ordained but not to the Ministry of Word and Sacraments. Lutheranism has been satisfied with a dual pastoral ministry – bishop/superintendent and local pastor, and Methodism bears strong similarities to it, though often combining both roles in one person. Baptists are a law unto themselves, but within the autonomy of many of their local congregations strong authoritarian figures, not to mention strong authoritarian families, arise and often 'rule'. As for Anglicanism, although the 1662 Book of Common Prayer claims that, 'It is evident .... that from the apostles' time there have been these orders of ministers in Christ's Church; bishops, priests and deacons,' the evidence is, like Calvin's, not overwhelmingly strong. '.... [these] words come from an ordinal which was supported by a parliamentary Act of Uniformity, trying to bring presbyterians and other dissenters to heel – what else could it say?' [6]

This is not the place to trace historical developments in 'episcopacy', that oversight of churches which was to manifest itself through popes, bishops, moderators, superintendents, ministers and the like; but some attention must be given to one of the main principles that lay behind all the arguments, for and against. What is clear, and what is affirmed by both the Church of Rome and the Reformed churches, is that there has been, from the apostles' time, ordered ministry – what in Roman Catholicism is referred to as the one sacrament of holy

---

6   Keith Riglin, my successor at St Columba's, Cambridge, in a paper at the Oxford Theology Summer School, 1999.

order (note the singular), albeit containing a two-fold or threefold division. It is this principle which seems most under threat in today's church because of an increasing *laissez-faire* attitude to ministry which, in its extreme manifestations, seems to be saying: 'Anything goes' and, in a less extreme form, 'Order is important, but not a priority today; let the Spirit blow where it will.'

To put it in its crudest form, the question is: Is the ministry 'from above' or 'from below'? For some, the ministry is 'from above', i.e. the gift of God to his Church. It is a way of being (ontological), rooted in both the ministry of Christ the 'great high priest' (Hebrews 4:14) and the priesthood of the whole Church, yet distinct within the Church through the gift of 'order' conveyed in ordination. On the contrary, others believe that the ministry is 'from below', i.e. it begins and ends with the setting apart by the people, as the Church, of particular persons to form or preside at certain rites within the community, sometimes within just one local congregation. Here the ministry, or simply 'ministry', is defined primarily, often exclusively, functionally – a way of doing. Like the ontological view, it claims roots in both Christ's ministry and that of the Church, often employing phrases such as 'the priesthood of all believers'. A rite called ordination may well be celebrated but, in intention, its emphasis is less on conveying order and more on the setting apart of certain persons to do certain things.

Sufficient has been said to underline that what Neuhaus said about the 'oddity' of the ministerial vocation owes more to the ontological view of ministry than to the functional one. It was previously argued that an ordered liturgy does not preclude 'free-er' patterns of worship, but is 'in order' so that the latter's centrifugal tendencies should be kept within reasonable bounds. The same plea must now be made where the Ministry of Word and Sacraments is concerned, and for similar reasons. This, of course, is not to deny the 'validity' of other less 'ordered' ministries, the fruits of which often speak for themselves.

Thus there are two main positions on the ordained ministry within Reformed theology which vie for predominance – the ontological and the functional. The differences between them give rise to real differences of opinion on important issues at the congregational and parish level: e.g. those of the ontological persuasion generally hold that, for order's sake, only the ordained person can preside at the sacrament; those on the functional side do not see this as essential. (The Basis of Union of my own church, the United Reformed Church, allows for lay presidency to be exercised 'where pastoral necessity so requires' – albeit a compromise-ruling which often comes up against the difficulty of defining what really constitutes 'pastoral necessity'.) [7]

The 1984 report of the Anglican-Reformed International Commission – 'God's Reign and Our Unity' – concludes: 'The general rule should remain that the president at the eucharist should be the person who has, by ordination, received the authority so to preside, and the Church ought to order its affairs in such a way that this proper rule may be kept. The presidency of the ordained person does not depend upon his (*sic*) possessing a priesthood which others lack; it depends upon the good ordering which is essential to the life of the Church as it exercises corporately the priesthood given to it by the one who is alone the good High Priest.' [8]

Keith Riglin, to whom I am indebted for pointing out this quotation, writes: 'It is an interesting conclusion, for it manages to combine a functional view of the ministry with a "high" view of ordination and the "essential" character of a Church well ordered.'

It would be satisfying to leave the matter on this irenic note were it not for two important issues that arise out of the above.

First, from my description at the beginning of this chapter, it is obvious that the minister of my mother's time and also, for that matter, of my youth, was certainly a focus for the congregation and the main representative of the Church to the world outside the congregation. In 1974, the British Methodist Conference issued a 'Statement on Ordination' in which these related notions of focus and representation were underlined: 'The idea is that the special or ordained ministry brings the multi-faceted ministry of the whole Church to sharp or concentrated expression in such a way that all Christians may be stimulated and enabled to exercise the Church's ministry – and that the whole Church's ministry may also

---

7   The Basis of Union of the United Reformed Church, paragraph 24.
8   God's Reign and Our Unity; report of the Anglican-Reformed International Commission 1984, p53.

be clearly identified by those yet outside the Church to whom the Gospel is being commended. The metaphor of focus indicates that the special ministry is not an exclusive ministry .... yet a focus is also distinctive, and this is confirmed by the notion of representation. The special character of the Ordained Ministry consists precisely in its being an efficacious sign in the furtherance of the divine purpose both in the Church and in the world to which the Church bears witness.' [9]

This would seem to denote a 'high' view of the ministry but, in my view, it is not quite 'high' enough and does not do full justice to the ontological nature of the ministry. Calvin, and others, stressed that the ministerial office was a *gift* from Christ, belonging to Him as the Head of the Church. It followed from this that ministerial 'powers' do not derive from the Church or its members, or from any other earthly source. The Call of the People does not confer the Ministerial Office; in that sense, therefore, the minister is not what we normally would describe as a representative figure. He is not primarily representing the congregation's opinions to the wider world and, by the same token, neither is he there simply to achieve some kind of common focus within the local church for those same opinions. He is an Ambassador of Christ to the people of God, a calling which is manifested through the exercise of the Ministry of Word and Sacraments, and which can often involve a prophetic ministry which runs counter to the views of those he has been called to serve. He represents Christ to the people, focusing their hearts and minds on Him, so that they can, in turn, represent Christ to the world.

None of this is to deny that the people have a vital say in his or her appointment. In many Reformed churches this principle is rightly adhered to and a minister has to be 'called' by the majority. It is a Call which has to be sustained by both the local presbytery/district council (or similar court or council) from which he/she comes, as well as by the one to which he/ she goes; usually, however no obstacle is put in the way.

There corresponds to all this an understanding of ordination as 'the laying on of hands' – by the presbytery or district council, but this is the point at which several of our churches give very mixed signals. The office-bearers should not act in the name of the people but simply as a result of their commission from Christ.

---

9   Statement of Ordination, British Methodist Conference 1974.

They are not ordaining the people's representative, but Christ's Ambassador, and he is certainly not the people's delegate! I think it was P T Forsyth who once stated: 'The Church does not shape the ministry, the ministry shapes the Church.' The people at an ordination are called upon to give their assent, but that is another matter.

All of the above does raise issues which, to some, might seem secondary, if not totally irrelevant. How, for instance, can a minister 'go public', and be recognised as such by that public, if he is not easily identifiable? The issue of the dog-collar can make some Christians very hot under theirs, clerical or otherwise. To some, it smacks of a certain understanding of the ministry which they feel would give the wrong signals, so best to do without it. In any case, many of those who feel this way do not set great store by the representative role of any one individual, seeing it as the responsibility of the whole church (which of course it is, but one does not exclude the other).

Some Reformed ministers have tried to solve the problem by wearing white ties, thereby avoiding any lingering misunderstanding that the old 'Roman' collar gave rise to. This may well help them to identify with, and be identified by, their own congregations, but there would be something radically wrong if the latter did not know them already! But it does nothing for the 'outsider's' perception who simply sees a man (women have their own equivalents) in a white tie, perhaps more reminiscent of the Mafia than a minister of the Gospel. I remember being at a special memorial service once with a friend who was from the old school. His clerical collar must have been three inches in depth which, admittedly, was a bit extreme. The service was led by several ministers; three of them were sporting white ties. My companion turned to me and spluttered: 'Are they the undertaker's assistants?'

A few years ago, I was the preacher at a large Southern Baptist Church in the USA, a denomination which prides itself on parity of ministry among all its members. It had three ministers, all of whom were with me in the vestry. They all wore ties with a piano motif displayed upon them. The most junior sported a simple upright piano of the old variety. The next one up in the pecking order had a baby-grand on his, whereas the senior minister's neck-wear was dominated by a grand piano – with the lid open! 'Status' will out, whether in traditional ways or otherwise.

En passant, and contrary to what some put forward as an argument in favour of the collar, I have rarely been stopped by anyone in the street in need of help, spiritual or otherwise. When it has happened, the accoster has usually been a little the worse for drink and/or requesting the train fare from Bristol to the Western Highlands where his mother has only two more days' breath left in her. The main spin-offs from going public in a dog-collar are hidden, even from the parson. It is at least a sign that the church is still around, whether a welcome one or not; and, on occasion, the sight of it has reminded some of that earlier baptism of theirs, perhaps even their confirmation and the promises they made all those years ago.

The mention, however, of those members of the public who 'accost' the parson in the street brings us to the second way in which the ministry tends to be mistakenly regarded by those outside the church and, all too often, by those within it as well.

In an article in the *Christian Century* (USA) headed 'Ministry is More Than a Helping Profession', the authors write: 'If the ministry is reduced to being primarily a helping profession, then parish clergy will also be destroyed by the presumption that all sincerely felt needs are legitimate needs. Ministry will be trivialised into the service of needs.' [10]

Ministers are often people who need to help people; we like to be liked and need to be needed, and our personal needs can sometimes become almost the *raison d'être* for our ministry, (Does any other profession contain so many members who go on fulfilling their customary role way beyond retirement?) It can, of course, be the only area today within which the minister can find any scope at all to be seen to be doing something. But people's needs run very deeply and, once immediate needs have been dealt with, others follow quickly in their wake – especially in an affluent society in which there is an ever-rising threshold of desire (which we define as 'need'); 'With no clear job description, no clear sense of purpose other than the meeting of people's needs, there is no possible way for the pastor to limit what people ask of the pastor.' [11]

---

10   Hauerwas and Willimon: Christian Century; March 15, 1989.
11   Ibid.

All this is not to ignore the important pastoral role of the minister, one that lies outside the scope of these pages. But whereas pastoral responsibilities are closely aligned to the minister's liturgical and preaching office, and are best contextualised by it, the meeting of needs in general knows no such bounds. We must remember, however, that we are the Servants of God, not his door-mats!

Ministers are not ordained to be 'need-meeters'. Of course we are faced in the gospels by one who healed the sick, comforted the mourner, fed the hungry, and attended to people's needs. But there is strong evidence that Jesus did not meet every need; indeed, he seemed to have escaped purposively from time to time from such encounters to avoid his ministry being altogether taken up with this and, as a result, being thrown off course.

The church at worship continues to be the acid test for the Ministry of Word and Sacraments. In our worship we tell and re-tell, and are held accountable to, the story concerning what God has done, is doing and will do. All ministry can be evaluated by one essential truth: How well does it enable people to be with God? This is the only legitimate use of the term 'enable' in regard to ministry.

'Almost everything a minister does can be an opportunity to orient people toward God. Visiting the sick can be much more than empathetic sharing (after all, anybody can do that, even people who don't believe in God) if seen as an occasion for orienting someone to God: pastors would do well to examine their schedules and ruthlessly delete any activity that doesn't help people to do that which they do in worship.' [12]

Our church lives in a buyer's market where the customer is king; what the customer wants the customer should get. Ministers who pander to this web of buying and selling may well wake up one day and perhaps hate themselves for it. We will lose some of our (potentially) best ministers to an early grave of cynicism and self-hate.

---

12   Ibid.

Ministers who determine to speak the truth – to reprove, correct, witness, interpret, remember God's story – can expect to be lonely occasionally. But it would be a loneliness evoked by being faithful rather than a loneliness produced by merely being accessible. To the extent that the church and its leaders are willing to be held accountable to the story which is the gospel, ministry can help create a people worthy to tell the story and to live it. Not the least of the ways in which this can be done is through the faithful preaching of the word. Not before time, we must turn to that now.

Chapter Fourteen

Proclamation Not Speculation

Proclamation Not Speculation

Leander E Keck, the former Dean at Yale University Divinity School, begins his book, *The Bible in the Pulpit*, with this paragraph: 'Every renewal of Christianity has been accompanied by a renewal of preaching. Each renewal of preaching, in turn, has rediscovered biblical preaching. Nineteen centuries of experience suggests clearly that unless there is a recovery of biblical preaching, the dissipation of the Christian faith will continue.' [1]

The emphasis that has been given so far to the importance of the Lord's Supper, and to a recovery of a weekly celebration of the same, must not be understood to be playing down the importance of the sermon or homily; far from it. The point has been made several times over that we must strive for a proper balance between the preached Word in the sermon and the acted Word in the Sacrament, and both are to be held within the larger context of the liturgy as a whole. This does mean that there is no longer a place for those lengthy sermons of a former age in relation to which the rest of the service often stood as both a mere preliminary and a hasty denouement; but it does not mean that the preparation of the Word by the preacher, ordained or lay, should be approached with any less seriousness than before.

I remember as a young boy during the holidays from school often making some noise or other in the house, with assistance from my younger brother. Many was the time when mother interrupted our play with: 'Hush dears, daddy is in his study.' I often wondered why my daddy never went out to work like other friends' daddies and, as a child, I never really did understand what occupied him at his desk in the manse from Monday to Friday, from 8am until noon. It was only as I grew older that I learned that much of his time there was spent preparing his two sermons for the following Sunday – never mind dealing with local pastoral, and wider administrative concerns.

---

1   Leander E Keck: The Bible in the Pulpit – The Renewal of Biblical Preaching; Nashville, Abingdon Press, 1978, p11.

David Gardner, whose help and advice I have mentioned earlier in my acknowledgements, on reading the above told me how, as another son of the manse, his experience had been similar. But in his case his father had put a door-knocker on the door of his study so that David could, '*in extremis*', try to gain access (*sic*). If there was no reply he did not dare enter.

It is a matter of some sadness to notice the look of amazed disbelief on the faces of younger ministers and some lay preachers today when such tales are related. It seems a very far cry from their experience and sense of priorities. Of course times have changed considerably and the pressures along with them, not least those brought about by dwindling numbers in the pews which often results in the minister having to be jack or jill of all trades. But none of this should excuse us from relegating preparation for the pulpit to Saturday evening or, as I have discovered on several occasions, to early on Sunday mornings!

Leander Keck states categorically: 'Unless biblical preaching is recovered, the church as a whole will continue to suffer from amnesia'[2]. That recovery cannot take place without a wrestling with the texts week-by-week, seeing them within their original context and letting God's Word speak through them His message for us today. The preacher is called upon to contend with the Bible story, the Church's story and his or her own personal story as he or she struggles to proclaim God's gracious and judging Word, Sunday by Sunday.

Anything less is to forget that the preaching of the Word to the Reformers was of sacramental moment, as it has been to many Reformed ministers ever since. Nothing that has been said so far about the importance of the eucharist should disguise the Reformers' conviction that there is also a sacramental efficacy in the preached word, even one that is relatively independent of the quality of the preaching or of the character of the preacher.

One scholar (Ernst Bizer) has argued that the heart of Luther's reformation was the twofold recognition that the Sacrament is to be understood from the Word and the Word has a sacramental character. This, I think, holds for Calvin

---

2   Ibid., p32.

also, as it does for myself. All of this should be a reminder to every minister of the Word what an awesome responsibility is ours.

But no matter how seriously the preacher takes the preparation of sermons, and no matter how highly he or she hones their preaching to as fine an art as they are able, there is always a danger of the subjectivity of personal speech taking over more than it should. It needs to be balanced by the 'objectivity' of the Sacrament which, in its turn, requires the preaching and readings and prayers to ensure it does not get out of hand and go off on a ceremonial tangent all on its fussy own. 'The sermon .... will have always to take account of the fact that it is not in itself the climactic event of worship but the opening up of the mystery of the Lord's Day assembly, which is finally constituted in its "sacrifice of praise and thanksgiving," normatively over bread and cup. Thus the sermon "textualises" the sacramental or non-sacramental Thanksgiving, and the Thanksgiving "contextualises" the sermon and its scripture.' [3]

A shift in this direction is taking place in some parts of the United States today, one which has gone hand in hand with a growing liturgical use of Scripture across denominational boundaries. It has embraced both Protestant and Roman Catholic churches through the introduction of two lectionaries (tables of readings) which have emerged in recent years and which have a great deal in common.

The Roman Catholic lectionary arose as a direct result of the Second Vatican Council's directive that: 'The treasures of the Bible are to be opened up more lavishly, so that a richer share in God's word may be provided for the faithful. In this way a more representative portion of holy Scripture will be read to the people in the course of a prescribed number of years.' [4]

Thus did the Council take into the life of the Roman Church the principal concern of the sixteenth-century Reformers regarding the central place of the Bible in the worship of the Catholic Church.

---

3   Horace T Allen Jun: Handbook for the Revised Common Lectionary; edited by Peter C Bower; Louisville, Kentucky, Westminster John Knox Press, 1996, p2.

4   Vatican Council II: Constitution on the Liturgy; Sancrosanctum Concilium – 4 Dec. 1963; trans. International Commission on English in the Liturgy, Documents on the Liturgy, 1963-1979: Conciliar, Papal and Curial Texts; Collegeville, Minn: Liturgical Press, 1982, para 51.

Spurred on by this example, American and some other Protestant scholars began to meet in a gathering called 'The Consultation on Common Texts'. The result of their considerable deliberations was the publication in 1992 of the *Revised Common Lectionary*, which has close associations with the Roman tables. This has now been published in the United Kingdom and is recommended for use by an increasing number of our church authorities, including the United Reformed Church in the United Kingdom and the Church of Scotland, both of whom have printed this lectionary in their own service books.

The Roman and Protestant lectionaries incorporate a similar three-year cycle of readings which provide every Sunday with lessons from the Hebrew Scriptures, followed by a Psalm, and then the Epistle and Gospel. There is such close agreement between the two that it is not uncommon in the United States to find weekly ecumenical groups of priests, ministers, church school teachers and others engaged together in the study of the texts for the ensuing Sunday. This pattern could provide a way forward for us in the United Kingdom as well, and deepen cooperation at the ecumenical level.

Horace Allen, who was one of the members of the original Consultation on Common Texts, has said with justifiable pride: 'Preachers throughout Australia, New Zealand, Canada, South Africa, South Korea, Great Britain and the United States are now being confronted and challenged by virtually the same biblical texts each week. There has not been such a wide agreement on readings since the break-up of Western Catholicism in and after the Sixteenth Century.'

(But, at the time of writing this chapter, there is a small, dark cloud appearing on the horizon. There is a debate at top level in the Roman Catholic Church concerning the translation of liturgical texts into English. There is a strong move afoot to revert to more traditional cadences. Also it is possible that the Roman Catholic Church will soon have its own translation of the Bible. It is possible that all this could affect the agreement just mentioned. Also, at the time of going to press, Pope Benedict XVI had only recently been elected to office, and his influence will be crucial.)

But if the present advances that have been made sound like a recipe for dull conformity and a stultifying homogeneity, nothing could be further from the case. But to support such a claim, we need to ask, and answer, the question: Why a lectionary anyway? Why lectionaries when we have managed without them since the Reformation? For it is certainly true that many of my contemporaries, myself included, were never trained, or recommended, to use set patterns of readings when it came to preparing for the pulpit and the sanctuary. We might be inclined to suggest that it was no handicap at all and left us more free to wait upon the Spirit's guidance. In fact, we did have a lectionary – the '*lectio selecta*' – the self-selection of readings. But I can remember the many hours spent flicking through the Bible wishing the Holy Spirit would make up his/her mind more quickly – especially when it got around to Thursday!

I have been using the present lectionary for several years from the time when it was, in experimental embryo form, circulated to enthusiasts like myself. Retirement has allowed me the leisure to look back over many of the sermons that were prepared in my pre-lectionary period and compare them with those which were *post hoc*. It would appear that, in the former state, I began thinking of Sunday by asking, 'What do I want to preach this time? What should my text be?'; whereas the later question became more akin to, 'What am I, as a servant of the scriptures and a presider at the sacraments, to say in the light of these readings?' One of H H Farmer's *bons mots* in sermon class was: 'Never begin a sermon by saying "*My* text is ....". It is not *your* text!'.

Many of us who have preached without the aid of a lectionary are not always aware, until it is too late, how narrowly selective our own readings and texts have been. With such freedom (licence?) it is very hard to avoid repetition of favourite passages and quite easy to avoid those we consider to be too difficult or irrelevant. This especially applies to passages in the Hebrew Scriptures, the use of which seems to have declined alarmingly in many of our churches today. There is a little Marcion in all of us struggling to get out. It was in the middle years of the second century that this first radical reformer of the church appeared. Marcion undertook to purify the church of its Jewish elements because he was convinced that Jesus came to save humanity from Judaism and its God, the creator and law-giver. He was very successful for a time.

The trend towards self-selection even spread to Martin Luther with his desire to purge the Epistle of James from the New Testament canon. This process of de-selection has found its supporters among many preachers and teachers since, consciously or otherwise.

The result has often been to make the subject of the sermon condition which lessons are selected, rather than the scriptures providing the context which controls the preaching. This practice has found its logical conclusion in the unsatisfactory, but growing, habit of 'theme' preaching and 'theme' services. A theme is thought up by the leader of worship, or taken from a book of aids to worship, and the scriptures are slotted in to serve the theme.

I groan, and not always inwardly, when I enter a church today on either side of the Atlantic, and see at the head of the bulletin sheet that 'the theme today' is such and such. It does not take long, by noting the printed lessons and hymns, to work out in advance the predictable course the service will take. Straight away one's expectations are narrowed, lessened by the awareness of the theme; and the element of surprise, which can often strike an awakening chord during a service (sometimes literally!), will be absent. The same applies to the largely American custom of sermon titles which are often pre-published in Saturday's local paper, giving an even longer time for the potential worshipper to work out what will be going on and to avow to give it a miss; this, of course, is the opposite of what is intended.

The late Professor James Stewart, a much admired preacher of the middle of the twentieth century, says somewhere words to the effect that when he began his ministry as a young man in Scotland, he would sit down each Monday morning in his study and say to himself, 'What shall I preach on this Sunday?' He would then think of a subject, perhaps 'peace' or 'forgiveness' or 'justice' or the like, and then set to with a will. But after a few months he discovered that he was running out of subjects. Only then did he recall his college training and returned to the scriptures as his starting point. Very soon it came as a pleasant surprise that he could now preach the following Sunday on 'peace' and, with a different text, preach again on 'peace' the Sunday after that if he had a mind to, and so on. Each occasion still left much more that could have been said.

Sermons arising out of the Word which God speaks through the scriptures are open-ended in a way which it is impossible for a theme to be. The effect of the sermon is meant to extend beyond its actual delivery; the preaching enterprise is unfinished business as it feeds from the scriptures and into the Sacrament, all three elements being of equal significance for the task of Christian formation. We have to leave the people to write their own conclusions to gospel address, often taking from it a message and a challenge that the preacher had never imagined had been touched upon at all. The art of preaching must resist premature foreclosure in a way that theme preaching and theme services are unable to do. As one experienced minister friend of mine put it: 'People have to be lured into the drama and find themselves on stage.'

It has been unfortunate in this regard that, in the new lectionary, the existence of the three main lessons for each Sunday has given rise to the misunderstanding that they have been chosen because they are united by a common theme. In some instances a common thread is apparent, but not in the majority of cases. They are, on the whole, designed to be read sequentially, following each other week by week over a set period of the Christian year – Hebrew Scriptures and Gospel lessons following in a continuous, serial fashion. This follows the ancient tradition of the synagogue and was practiced and advocated by John Calvin.

Obviously, the Gospel lesson has some priority (though not, as we have noticed, in certain churches judging by its premature position or non-position in some services) and needs some sort of homiletic use; this does not mean that the text should only be drawn from the Gospel, but that perhaps it should at least be used as illustration in the course of the sermon. The other lessons, however, are not meant to be forced into thematic agreement – this would be to end up with the worst of all worlds. Nor should the preacher preach three brief disconnected homilies. The Holy Spirit can be trusted to speak through a passage that is read publicly even if it is not expounded in the sermon. (Calvin spoke of the 'testimony of the Holy Spirit' and the 'plain meaning of the Scripture'.)

It could be conceded that special Sundays of the Christian Year do have specific themes, as at Easter, Pentecost and Christmas. But this is not the case with the more numerous Sundays of Ordinary Time, as they are now called. These

Sundays do not have different 'themes'; they have one theme: the whole Gospel as a 'witness to his resurrection' (Acts 1:22). That is why, in the Revised Common Lectionary, the reading from the Epistles on these Sundays is not thematically coordinated with the Gospel. The Epistles were written *to* the churches, those first 'witnesses to the Resurrection'. What has a theme to do with a sermon anyway? That is to transform proclamation into speculation.

The bureaucracies of our churches have much to answer for when it comes to this matter of themes and topics by setting apart, as they do, special Sundays throughout the year for the heightening of awareness and concern for particular enterprises – everything from Christian Education to Senior Citizen Sundays. In some quarters it is done to such an extent that it is a wonder that Easter and Pentecost and other major festivals of the Christian Year get a look in at all! It can get out of hand as the following story illustrates.

A friend of mine was an official in one of the leading Protestant denominations in the United States in the Seventies and was a member of a special committee which, each October, drew up the list of topics for the ensuing year's fifty two Sundays. The final draft was about to be agreed and sent to the printer when my friend, who had recognised the anomaly but had waited to see if he alone had done so, pointed out to the committee that they had decided to designate December 25th, which happened to fall on the Lord's Day that year, as 'Youth Appreciation Sunday'!

It is right that we should be concerned to bring to the notice of the people of God many important matters, but to make them the subject of whole services and sermons is to do the issues themselves less than justice. But if, like James Stewart, we begin from the biblical context and text, we could find ourselves in the course of a year dealing with issues such as Peace and Justice, Christian Education, Age Concern and all the rest several times over, and not just on a one-off occasion; in any case, our starting point lies elsewhere. William Maxwell, writing at the time of the Second World War, in the midst of the all-consuming trauma of those days, could still observe: '(The minister) will consistently teach the people that they come to divine worship in order to offer and to give, to pay honour and fealty to Almighty God, and not merely to receive guidance, comfort, and inspiration, although these are among the fruits of worship. He will direct their thoughts towards the majesty and glory of God, and quicken their sense of duty towards Him. Sermons should contain evangelical and moral appeals, but also be systematic expositions of Holy Scripture and Christian doctrine, calculated not only to draw men (*sic*) to Christ, but also to build them up in the Faith and make them full men in Christ. The clergy should be humbly and deeply conscious of the sacredness of their calling as Ministers of Jesus Christ, and stewards of the mysteries of God.' [5]

Themes and personal needs can be dealt with better if, first, we are caught up in sacred worship, the 'fruits' of which no-one can foresee but which can be of surprising relevance to our world and ourselves.

The presuppositions which many Protestant churches manifest today concerning the priority of thematic services, thematic preaching and an unsystematic use of scriptures, provide very shaky foundations for the commitment to the proclamation of the Word in all its fullness. Its proclamation cannot be fully served by the preacher in the sermon alone, but by the content of the whole service – praise, readings, prayers – with its eucharistic climax. The preacher has to pay close attention to these important beginnings and endings, and shape his or her preaching accordingly. It is interesting to note that all the readings in the *Revised Common Lectionary* take for granted that they will find their final outworking beyond the preached Word to the acted one at the table.

Such a schema is not escapist, or irrelevant, to the social and political scene, which we often seem to think can only be covered by a thematic approach. We make the mistake of thinking that it is only the sermon which can raise social/ ethical 'issues' – thus putting the onus on the preacher and his or her abilities and personal preferences. But when the preacher as presider is under the discipline of the set texts, and when his or her preaching leads into the Sacrament, the sermon takes place within a context which makes it very difficult for such 'issues' (as opposed to 'themes') to be avoided. The Wesleyan revival certainly had its own ethical as well as eucharistic dimensions. The Oxford Movement in the Church of England was the same, as a reading of A G Hebert's *Liturgy and Society* demonstrates. [6]

---

5   op.cit. pp68-69.
6   A G Hebert: Liturgy and Society; London, Faber, 1935.

One of the strategic mistakes of American liberal Protestantism of the 1960's and '70's was that it was largely non-liturgical, individually-motivated and uninterested in ecclesial structures except as validating support systems. The same was not true on the Catholic side, as many of the activists in the Civil Rights Movement were also liturgical reformers. Liberal Protestantism had, at best, its denominational 'backing' and its own personal commitments. It did not, however, nor could it in the nature of things, have the inevitable and unfailing communal participation in rites of solidarity, communion and sacrifice. All it had were sermons which were either 'for' or 'against', and either 'agreed' or 'disagreed' with the matter in hand.

Even though it seems to be only sermons which can raise social/ethical 'issues', it is 'Supper-as-love-feast', and 'Baptism-as-initiation' which forms the kind of intentional communities which, by their cult, become counter-cultural – can speak against the prevailing views of the day. Of course, that was precisely the experience of the Jewish diaspora synagogue, and also of the early Christian eucharistic communities in such places as Rome, Lyons, Canterbury and Iona. All this is not to underestimate the place of preaching in the liturgy; rather is it to see it in its liturgical context, one which should empower it rather than weaken it. But, faced with the liturgical fact that the Word-Sacrament unity is still not a regular occurrence in many of our Reformed churches, where do we begin?

The possible solution to this problem has already been touched upon, and there should be no need to add to it. Much, however, does depend upon the willingness of the presider at worship to shape his or her own consciousness on the basis of the Word-Sacrament continuum. In the absence of the Sacrament, we should at least ensure that after the sermon there is not only the final hymn and benediction, but a rite of offering and thanksgiving, followed by a hymn of triumphant praise. This 'action' should not be a rushed foreclosure, but stand on its own as an integral third part of the service.

The perceptions of the congregation, in this regard, could be furthered even more by the 'furnishing' of the Lord's Table at all times; that is, to place on them every Sunday the chalice and the patten, maybe with a loaf of bread and the cup filled with wine. The Bible does not belong on the Table, its place is in the pulpit and/or the lectern; far less do the minister's notes, spectacles, along with microphone, reading plinth and flowers, belong there either. I have even seen a hand-bag dominating the Holy Table – 'A hand-bag!' I can hear Lady Bracknell exclaim! [7]

One would hope, by such means, that the people of God may be gently led to see for themselves the necessity for the preaching of God's Word to find its natural climax in the weekly gathering around the Table of the Lord and, beyond, their calling to engage in a deeper commitment to God's world.

---

7   Oscar Wilde: 'The Importance of Being Earnest'.

Chapter Fifteen

What about the Children?

What about the Children?

Children are both the church of tomorrow and an important part of the church family at worship today, but so far they have not received a mention. The next two chapters are meant to make amends, but first we must look at the ways in which many Reformed churches endeavour to attract and hold the interest of the young within the context of morning worship.

Children are present usually because their parents have brought them or, less likely, have sent them. It is unusual to find those who have come on their own initiative, unless it happens to be a parade service for the uniformed organizations. Their presence is recognised via the medium of what is called the 'Children's Address' or 'Family Time' or 'All-Age Worship'. Apart from the latter, which often occupies the whole service, the first two methods usually involve a five to ten minute slot during the first quarter of the service. This time is given over to a talk, or visual presentation, the prime aim of which is to hold the attention of the young and, one hopes, to communicate a message. Although the minister or leader may not be successful in fulfilling this aim, he or she can rest assured that at least it is the part of the service to which some of the adults look forward the most!

Occasionally, when I have been visiting members of former congregations where I had been the minister, some have mentioned approvingly what they thought was a sermon they had heard me preach several years before. It has always caused some amusement when I tell them that what they were actually remembering was the children's talk and not the sermon. But there are good reasons for this.

'Why is it, after all, that the children's address retains its inalienable hold on congregational affection and memory, whatever may be its actual reception by the age-group for which it was ostensibly intended? It is not because it communicates significant truth. Characteristically, its message may be trivial, jejune, and dubiously Gospel. It is not because it necessarily and of itself communicates in any clear and particular direction at all. Characteristically, it may require the explanatory moral punch line to uncover the lesson supposed to be drawn. It is not even because of the natural human love of reviving buried memories of lost youth on the one hand, and of seeing ministers behave in avuncular fashion on the other. It surely has profounder roots. They are of a piece with those of the preaching use of illustration. In a curious way, but with a deeply right instinct, the congregation is sighing for what is denied, saluting a pale adumbration of what the sermon ought to be: narrative, dialogue, story, suspense, movement, all creative of the expectancy of the yet-to-be revealed.' [1]

Neville Clark's insight is painfully accurate, but the implications are more relevant to better sermon construction than an imprimatur to continue with present practices where our young folk are concerned.

A keen church-goer was trying to persuade a friend to come to his church. By way of inducement he said, 'Our minister gives wonderful children's talks and you will at least enjoy that part of the service.' The friend allowed himself to be coerced and went along the following Sunday. After the service his host enthused, 'Did you enjoy the children's talk?' – to which he answered sardonically, 'Yes – both of them'!

I write as one who spent most of his ministry in following the well-trodden path of trying to hold the children's interest either by telling a story or by presenting a visual aid (mainly the former) and if I could amuse them and the adults into the bargain, all well and good. In many Reformed churches this is set between the Old Testament Lesson and the second hymn. The latter is usually followed by the enthusiastic, and sometimes indecently hasty, departure of the children for the relative freedom of the Junior Church. On the occasions when we had a very young constituency to deal with, the strategy of bringing them to sit in the chancel at the minister's feet was also pursued. This could make for a feeling of intimacy between both parties but, as the adults could only see and hear the children with difficulty, it failed to draw them into its ambience in the way that the more conventional approach sometimes did. Throughout all these procedures, however, I felt a profound unease.

---

1   Neville Clark: Preaching in Context; Bury St Edmunds, Kevin Mayhew Ltd, 1991, pp91-92.

It was relatively easy to hold their attention provided the story was a good one or the visual aid was enthralling; it was quite another matter to make an effective Gospel and adequate Faith point out of any of it, and to make one that was not stiflingly moralistic into the bargain. All of us who have undergone this experience have dreaded reaching that point of no return, the point when the 'entertainment' stops and the application begins. The shuffling of feet, the whispered conversations in front of you, even the occasional fight that broke out in front of me on the chancel steps, were all a warning that by this time you were talking to yourself, and the pressure was truly on how to bring about a speedy foreclosure and a relieved announcement of the next hymn.

There are ministers who spend the whole week in dread of this moment and find it the most difficult part of their preparation for the morning worship. But the burden upon them can be lessened if, through faithfully exercising their pastoral ministry, the children of the church already know them as people who have visited them in their homes, and have made the attempt to relate to them there. They are more likely, on a Sunday morning, to respond, even help their pastor out on those occasions when he or she seems to be getting nowhere fast. Continuity of pastoral relationship can be far more effective in the long run in influencing the young to reach the deep things of the faith if it is grounded in, and flows from, the Sunday liturgy. Why continue, then, with the children's address?

Dick Shepherd, the charismatic vicar of St Martin-in-the-Fields, London, after the First World War, had an interesting habit whenever he was on his annual summer vacation, often spent in parts of rural England. He would go into every parish church he could and, if there were any copies of the latest edition of the parish magazine lying around, he would take them away and destroy them 'before they could do any more damage'! It will sound a little cynical to say the least, but perhaps a similar ruthlessness is called for where our talks to the young are concerned.

Richard Neuhaus has some observations which reinforce the point being made. In the course of talking about visual aids and 'other gimcrackery' (*sic*) in the sanctuary, he writes: 'Such nonsense is not experiment with, but abandonment of, preaching .... Such visual tricks are too often used in a pitch to the children. Many adults will say that they prefer the 'children's sermons', with its little toys and tricks, but that is a preference not to be pandered to. There is a perilous cuteness about doing things for the kiddies in church. Some adults are entertained by it, but entertainment is a far remove from serious engagement in the proclamation of the Word. Preachers should resist the temptation to gain the attention of the parents by gaining the attention of their children, for what that usually means is that parental attention is focused not on the sermon but on the phenomenon of their children paying attention .... But it is much better for the children's attention to be held in church by the phenomenon of attentive adults; children should be able to see that *worship is a communal venture they grow up into, not a kiddies hour they grow out of.* [2]

Michael Ignatieff, describing his family history, focuses on his grandparents who fled with their young sons from the Russian Revolution to Canada. Ignatieff was born of one of these sons in Toronto. He writes: 'I heard very little Russian as a child: my father did not speak it at home, [but] .... I went with him to the Russian church in the cities where I grew up – New York, Toronto, Ottawa, Belgrade, Paris, Geneva and London – and I was moved by the service because I did not understand it. Standing beside him in the church, watching him light his candles, say his prayers and sing in his deep vibrating voice, I always felt that he had slipped away through some invisible door in the air.' [3]

Ignatieff's experience seems to have been akin to that of mine described in chapter one – an experience of the majesty of God. It was certainly not dependent on any 'gimcrackery' or, to be more charitable, the well-meaning attempts of my father, and others, to hold my attention. Neuhaus suggests that if there are parts of the service that elude the seven-year-old, that is no fault. He makes the interesting suggestion that perhaps families might even be encouraged to revive the custom in which the sermon was regularly discussed afterwards at home, and then parents can explain what the children missed. But I fear that in our present secular climate, when even Sunday dinner is not the cohesive force it once was, circumstances and life-styles would get the better now of any effort to implement this.

---

2   Neuhaus: op.cit. pp188-189 (my italics).
3   Michael Ignatieff: The Russian Album; London, Vintage Press, 1997, p11.

The overall long-term solution is not easy. But I do not think it lies with what, today, is called: 'All-Age Worship', unless we define this term more carefully than we do. I must confess that when I see publicised that a service is an 'All-Age' one, I give it a miss, and I am not alone in my reaction. Occasional forays into their midst have only confirmed my suspicions that most are at the level of the children's address, but now extended to an hour's length. It is difficult to see how any casual worshipper, coming out of a sense of need or, for that matter, gratitude, could find much which would encourage them to return.

This will, no doubt, seem a very harsh judgement on many well-meaning attempts (sometimes very successful ones) to engage the attention of the children for a longer span than usual and may, in part, be the result of my own lack of expertise where such services are concerned. A great deal of time and thought often goes into their preparation and there are some very commendable publications from church departments and other sources which provide useful material and ideas.

None of the above reservations mean that there is no room for services which accommodate the presence of children through a longer time span than is customary. The Christian Year supplies plenty of opportunities for this from Advent and Christmas right through to Pentecost, never mind the spectacle of the sacraments of Baptism and Communion with their potential for iconic influence on the young. These special festivals, with the opportunity they bring for an extended use of movement, colour, banners, special music and the like, should not be 'spoiled' by interrupting them with little talks to the children alone. Nor should they seek only to involve the youngsters in the action. To present a true 'all-age' act of worship we would have to ensure that, for instance, on a Palm Sunday it is not just the children who are carrying the palm-leaves around the church, but the adults as well.

It is all very well, however, to be citing the example of Michael Ignatieff as a child. His experience was within the Orthodox church where the icons, the incense, the candles and the *basso profundo* singing of cantor and choir, all serve to create an atmosphere which the Reformed churches could not begin to match, even if they wanted to. Nonetheless, lessons can be learned from the Orthodox understanding of the place of children in worship.

Thomas Hopko, an Orthodox theologian, writes as follows: 'The Orthodox Church over the centuries has consistently followed the practice of allowing baptised and chrismated [that is, anointed with oil immediately after baptism] children, including infants in arms, to participate in holy communion. This practice was originally not an exclusively Eastern one. There is ample evidence indicating that baptised children were brought to the altar for holy communion in the early Western Church as well. The cessation of this practice in the Middle Ages may be attributed to the clericalisation of the Church, the withdrawal of the eucharist generally from lay people (with the complete withdrawal of the chalice), and the triumph of a decadent scholastic theology. This Western medieval practice of forbidding baptised children to participate in the eucharist was retained with almost no exception in the Protestant churches.' [4]

Father Hopko makes it clear that, in the Orthodox view, children can and must be baptised if there are adult members of the Church, usually but not necessarily their parents, who will see that they are raised and nurtured in the faith and life of the Church. They are then brought to baptism, chrismation and holy communion from infancy 'so that they can grow and develop in the light and truth of Christ, by the grace and power of the Holy Spirit, from their earliest days.' [5]

He makes an entirely logical point when he compares critically the custom of the overwhelming majority of Christians in the Roman and Reformed churches who practise infant baptism while forbidding baptised infants and small children to have holy communion, although the Roman Catholic custom of confirmation as early as seven or eight permits quite young children to partake. He asserts that the Protestant position is illogical in maintaining that communion requires some sort of understanding and commitment which baptism does not. What he does not point out, however, is that it is not the custom within Orthodoxy for children to take communion on a regular weekly basis until they are at least five years old. In addition, there are many adults in the Orthodox churches who do not receive it on a regular basis either.

---

4   Thomas Hopko: All the Fullness of God; Crestwood, New York, St Vladimir's Seminary Press, 1982, p129
5   Ibid., p131

I must confess to a feeling of unease at this point having, for much of my ministry, either come down on the side of those who believe children should wait until they reach some understanding of what communion is about, or simply side-stepped the issue altogether; I am not alone,and I am still not really sure where I stand on the matter. Some of my hesitations are based on non-theological pragmatic grounds – giving bread and wine to a baby, or even a toddler, sounds very much like force-feeding; not an attractive prospect! Also, how can we expect children to participate in a way that does not distract the rest of us from the 'serious' business in hand? Are they not prone to fidget, even to shout and scream – the very tiny ones anyway – when their presence is prolonged beyond the ten or fifteen minutes to which they have normally been accustomed? How many sermons have been ruined for others simply because an indulgent mother and father have decided unilaterally to keep their child with them throughout a service, no matter the cacophony emanating from the bundle in their arms or the toddlers playing at their feet? Our irritation has often been compounded by how oblivious some such parents seem to be to the annoyance caused. Even when grim faces turn their way they smile back, mistaken in their belief that we can hardly wait to get close to their little darling. In one sense, they are right!

This kind of argument could also be used to deny children access to the family meal table in the home. That such access is, thankfully, not denied in the majority of cases is because parents recognise that they have a responsibility at such times to exercise both a modicum of control and also to ensure that their children are properly nourished and included, not withstanding the fact that today's children do not always eat the same food, even at family meals. If they behave in a way that discomforts others, then they can be removed for a while. Should not this responsibility be joyfully replicated when such parents and their offspring gather with the larger family on the Lord's Day for the Lord's Supper?

I have less difficulty over the objection about the children's inability to understand what is going on at the Sacrament. After all, which one of us could claim that we have full understanding at this point? We have already shown that many in the Reformed tradition have misunderstood what the Sacrament is about at very crucial levels. It could even be argued that children have an advantage over the average adult, albeit at an entirely intuitive level.

In his First Letter to the Corinthians St Paul writes: 'For all who eat and drink without discerning the body, eat and drink judgement against themselves.' (I Corinthians 11:29). C K Barrett translates the Greek by 'distinguish', with the implication that the communicant's fault is a failure to perceive, and to give due weight to, the presence of the rest of the assembly as members one of another in Christ. [6] Moffatt translates the meaning as: 'Without a proper sense of the body'. Children can have this ability to 'discern/distinguish/sense' the presence of fellow Christians, just as much as any adult, sometimes more so.

But many manuscripts add 'Lord', resulting in the reading: 'If he does not discern the Lord's body.' This, however, does not alter the point being made concerning the intuitive ability of the child. St Matthew records that, in the temple, the blind and the crippled came to Jesus and he healed them. When the chief priests and scribes saw what was happening they were indignant, but it was the young children in the temple who saw what was really going on, and who Jesus was: 'Hosanna to the Son of David!' they shouted, (Matthew 21:14) and Jesus acknowledged their insight, denied to the adults: '.... have you never read, "Out of the mouths of infants and nursing babies you have prepared praise for yourself"?' (Matthew 21:16).

Children do have this intuitive capacity to sense that something important is going on, and that we are all involved in it: 'Small children certainly know that something is happening around them and to them in the eucharistic worship of the church, particularly in their participation in holy communion. They know this as much as they know that something happens at home when they are carried, kissed and fed. Infants have minds as well as sensations and feelings. Their minds develop as they grow, interpreting and evaluating their sensible and emotional experiences.' [7]

Again, in the Reformed tradition, we cannot compete with Orthodoxy when it comes to sheer theatre, display and colour, which must seem like magic, in the best sense of the word, to little children. If you have ever, for instance, watched their faces when confronted with flickering candles in a warm church at Christmas, you will have an inkling of what I mean. Nonetheless I do believe we can provide

---

6   C K Barrett: First Epistle to the Corinthians; London, Adam and Charles Black, 1968, pp273ff.
7   Hopko: op.cit. p141.

an atmosphere for our children, as well as the adults, which does exercise a strong fascination for one and all, and which through ordered liturgy, conjoined with colour and movement and song, can succeed in ways which no amount of our more usual visual 'aids' and 'little talks', so frequently on offer, can ever hope to do.

I recognise that I am side-stepping important theological issues in what has been said. In the last few years debate has intensified around the questions of infant versus believers' baptism, the place of confirmation (is it necessary? does it not imply that baptism is somehow incomplete? etc.), and the growing practice of holding a service of Affirmation of Baptism as distinct from Confirmation. (The American Episcopal Church was the first major Church to opt for a pattern of complete initiation of infants, to which they added an optional and fully repeatable service of 'Affirmation' to be celebrated after the baptised infants had reached the age of discretion.) Then, arising out of all this, there is the over-arching question of the relationship of faith to understanding which we have just touched upon.

Again, we have to be careful not to define faith and understanding in purely intellectual terms. In many of our churches the impression has been given that the reception of Communion (which was to take place only after reaching the age of discretion) is conditional on the intellectual understanding involved: 'The fact that Communion was supposed to be a mystery (and that consequently only God and his Incarnate Son were likely to be capable of a full intellectual understanding of it) was never taken into account. No one had as yet worked out that there are many ways of learning and that the mere imparting of information has never been among the most successful ones. In point of fact, there are many people today who have no idea of the difference between education, nurture and formation'. [8]

There are to be found, however, churches which are quite imaginative in their efforts to involve children more totally in worship, short of actually giving them communion. The custom, in Anglican and Roman Catholic churches, of giving children a blessing at the altar is a prime example and it can be very moving to observe. The going up for a blessing cannot, of course, take place in those Reformed churches where the elements are passed along the pews; but fathers and mothers are capable, I would hope, of making their off-spring feel that this is a very

---

8   Forrester, McDonald, and Tellini: Encounter with God; Edinburgh, T & T Clark, 1996, pp129-130.

special moment together – perhaps they could hold each other and say a prayer together. This could be a vivid demonstration of the priesthood of all believers in action. It has been suggested that if the children are baptised, it could be up to the discretion of the parents concerned whether their children take the Sacrament or not. There is also no reason why youngsters should not assist, in those Reformed churches with a Great Entrance, in helping the elders carry the bread, wine and offering to the Table, perhaps with their parents as well.

Saying 'it has been suggested' could indicate once again my sitting-on-the-fence posture. Perhaps this is the case, but I would plead that it is due more to the confusion still remaining in my own mind. I am not, however, confused about the need for strenuous attempts to make children always feel at home in the House of the Lord and, above all, to expose them to worship which is *a communal venture they grow up into, not a kiddies hour they grow out of*. Donald Nicholl writes: 'How can you live in accordance with the teaching about being children if you are for ever hiding yourself away from children?', and he argues that this reinforces the need for theology to be done in the kind of human community 'where men and women are together, and …. where children are not hidden away.' [9]

All the above is not to overlook the need for a high standard of teaching and educational programmes in the Junior Church or Sunday School. This means that, unless their programmes take place at a different hour, the children must leave the service for a part of the time for this purpose. It is imperative that our children have the opportunity to learn the biblical stories which are foundational to the Faith and, through them, be drawn into the Story behind all these individual stories – the Story of our Creation and Redemption, the Story of the Love of God for us as it has been shown forth supremely in the life, death and resurrection of Jesus.

They will not hear such in our schools to the same extent as used to be the case, if they hear them at all, and a half-hour in Junior Church should be much more effective in the cause of Christian foundation than any 'chat' from the chancel steps.

---

9   Donald Nicholl: Is there a locus classicus for theology? In: The Beatitude of Truth: Reflections of a Lifetime:, London, Darton, Longman and Todd, 1997, pp52-64. Quoted by Rowan Williams in: Christ on Trial: How the Gospel Unsettles our Judgement; London, Harper Collins, 2000, p63. See also Rowan Williams: Lost Icons: Reflections on Cultural Bereavement; Edinburgh T and T Clark, 2000, Chapter 1.

Prior to going to the Junior Church, the young people should experience an opening act of worship which conveys something of the majesty and love of God. The 'natural break' from all this in Junior Church can then make them more receptive, on their return, to what is going on at the Table of the Lord. Even if the Sacrament is not celebrated on a weekly basis, the concluding note of thanksgiving, followed by the commission to go and serve the Lord, and then the blessing, is not a bad substitute (as a temporary measure, of course!).

When we are thinking about children in worship, we need perhaps to consider the matter in a little more depth.

Chapter Sixteen

Reforming Childish Religion

Reforming Childish Religion

Hear, O Israel: The Lord is our God, the Lord alone. You shall love the Lord your God with all your heart, and with all your soul, and with all your might. Keep these words that I am commanding you today in your heart. Recite them to your children and talk about them when you are at home and when you are away, when you lie down and when you rise. Bind them as a sign on your hand, fix them as an emblem on your forehead, and write them on the doorposts of your house and on your gates.

Deuteronomy 6:4-9

Jews call these words the *Shema*, from the opening Hebrew word translated 'Hear'. C Ellis Nelson, an American author, teacher, and Christian educator, in an article in the *Faculty Journal of Austin Seminary, Texas*, set out definitive guidelines for congregations and parents based upon research focused on when and how children learn basic religious practices and beliefs. He writes: 'During the recent past there has been an enormous expansion of knowledge about the way children learn and how what they learn relates to their personal development. My view of this research has left me with two conclusions of importance to church leaders. One is that very little research contradicts the process by which children form an image of God as described in the Shema. The other conclusion is that the implications of recent research about children's learning linked with the wisdom of the Shema is ignored by most mainstream Protestant churches. In truth, the most important influence in the formation of children's belief in God is their relation to parents and the practice of religion in the home. For this influence to be theologically mature, parents and other adults must participate in a congregation that is seeking to know the mind of Christ, an activity of study and practice that engages adults as well as children and youth.'[1]

---

1   C Ellis Nelson in 'Insights' – Spring 2002: Austin Presbyterian Theological Seminary; p3.

Sad to say, I am sure that Professor Nelson is right to hint at the present lack of actual teaching in the home, of an absence in Christian families of a modern equivalent of the pattern laid down in the Shema. Modern research does not actually contradict the process by which children form an image of God (as described in the Shema) but there are aspects of modern research which balk at the idea of a directive approach implied by the Shema, as opposed to a so-called non-directive approach. They would condemn this process as 'brain-washing' or, at a more sophisticated level, as being too directive, not to mention authoritarian. If we want our children to form an image of God, (to which many protesters would object anyway), at least, they might suggest, let it be brought about through a non-directive approach, one in which the children have to find out for themselves who God is (if he is at all!), and be left to make up their own minds one way or another.

It is a bit like the primary class who were given permission to draw a picture of anything they liked, and they set to energetically. The teacher walked around to see what progress was being made. She was rather puzzled by Mary's half-finished drawing:
'What is this supposed to be?' she asked gently.
'It is God, miss.'
'But no one knows what God is like.'
'They will when I have finished', said Mary triumphantly.

The methodology exemplified by the Shema would seem to some to signify too much of a directive approach, with its 'top-down' emphasis, as opposed to a non-directive one where the stress is more on being left to work out things for yourself. I have had personal experience of the tension that can arise when these two methodologies enter on a collision course with each other, as the following will illustrate.

Reference has already been made to the modern passion play, *A Man Dies*, which was performed in the 1960's by more than 200 youngsters in the church where I was minister (chapter 4 page 25). This could not have happened had we not got a large constituency to draw upon but, with over 600 teenagers on the books, this was not a problem. I cannot claim that such numbers were a result of any outstanding charisma on the part of the church leadership. In those days leisure facilities for anyone, far less the young, were practically non-existent on the post Second World War council house estates that were then erected throughout the United Kingdom on the fringes of our cities.

We, however, were fortunate enough to have a brand new set of buildings courtesy of the funds that the government made available to help replace buildings destroyed by enemy action, as had been the fate of the original St James's Church in the city centre. After much discussion, the elders and congregation agreed to open up the facilities every week-night for the benefit of young people. The response was almost overwhelming but, with the help of several dedicated men and women, we somehow managed.

Then came the decision to open the premises on Sunday evenings as well, one taken after a great deal of heart-searching. An important condition, however, was put in place. If a boy or girl wished to attend the Sunday night club they had to attend the evening service first. It did not seem unreasonable to me, nor to the majority of the elders, but up went the cry from several sources – not least from some of the youngsters themselves – 'It's bribery!' In a sense they were right, but I still maintain it was not corruption – and it worked. Problems certainly arose, ones which revolved around inappropriate behaviour during the evening worship and how to present a liturgy which was both faithful to the Reformed tradition but, at the same time, reasonably attractive to this unusual constituency. [2]

It worked, but only because of the directive approach which had been involved in its maturation. But I never had any doubt, at that time or since, about its legitimacy. After all, we were a church with a message to proclaim, a truth to communicate, and to do so in a missionary situation where, unlike the little girl, not many could have begun to sketch in even a rough outline of a divine image. They had to be brought within the orbit of church teaching and Christian education and, bringing very little knowledge of such with them, we had to start from basics, basics which, paradoxically, had to come from the 'top' down.

---

2   See Odds Against by Ernest Marvin, London, SCM Press, 1967, chapter 3: Liturgy – the work of the People.

I am unable to claim that many of those youngsters eventually became confirmed as full members of the church, but some did who otherwise would have not. And over the years a considerable number expressed their gratitude for the strong experiences they had then, both through the passion play and the worship. Indeed a few are now in full-time ministry. But that particular scenario could not last.

The reasons for this were both sociological and 'philosophical'. A decline of sorts in the club occurred once the estate had settled down. With the rebuilding of the city centre there came the arrival of competing social facilities such as cinemas, sophisticated dance halls, eateries (the Berni steak inns in Bristol were the forerunners of many similar ones throughout the country), pubs and an ice rink. The accessibility of all these, and more, was facilitated by the setting up of a modern transport system which brought the city centre within easy reach for one and all. Our facilities, not bedraggled by any means, were no match for such competition.

There was another factor which made it very difficult to hold fast to the course we were on, and it was a threat from within! It came from those who, though not hostile to what we stood for, preferred to go about things in a more non-directive way.

In 1960 the Albemarle Report was published, taking its name from the chair person – the Countess of Albermarle – of the commission set up by the government to look at the whole question of youth work throughout the country. One of its major recommendations was to urge the government to put youth work and the training of full-time youth workers onto a more professional basis, and to provide the appropriate facilities and training for this. It was a much needed requirement and the nation has since benefited greatly from the implementation of the Report, though in ways we have now taken for granted. At first we thought we had gained a very great deal because, eventually, we were assigned two full-time youth leaders paid for by the local authority.

But this is where the 'philosophical' factor, brought by these newly trained arrivals, became a 'threat' to the way we were used to working. Their approach, as a result of their training, was of a largely non-directive order, and to try to marry it with the existing directive regime proved to be impossible. It was complicated by the fact that the two persons concerned were agnostic as far as the things of the Faith were concerned. (I don't think St Paul had future youth work in mind when he warned against being 'mismatched with unbelievers' (II Corinthians 6:14 NRSV) but he had a point!).

A book published at the time [3] was seminal to the thinking of the young (mainly) men and women who were trained in the new ways at that time. In it the Battens underlined how the traditional approach to social betterment had been directive in the sense that most social development agencies had aimed at getting people to accept the agencies' own preconceived ideas of what was good for them (as we were doing in Bristol!). They acknowledged that this approach had proved beneficial in certain areas but went on to praise those agencies which had experimented with a quite different approach – the non-directive or community development approach in which the agency no longer tries to persuade people to accept any preconceived ideas of its own. It aims, moreover, at stimulating them to clarify and define their own needs for themselves and then to decide and plan what they themselves can do to meet them. I think the devotees of this method were inclined to ignore the qualifications which the Battens themselves made about it, just as I was slow to see the merits it did have.

Of course, no matter how skilled we as a church might have become in practising the non-directive method (e.g. in getting the young folk to discuss their needs as far as the club was concerned and deciding how best to take action to meet those needs), the same methodology would have had no success whatsoever in providing a learning situation within which the tenets of the Faith would be communicated. Only direct teaching sufficed, and still does I believe, as the sole starting point for any possible growth into the Faith. The Sunday rule, which ensured a full attendance at worship, was never primarily intended as a means towards filling the hall afterwards. It was always seen as an opportunity to introduce the unchurched to the experience of worship and to the teaching that gives rise to, and underpins, that very same worship.

And so back to the Shema.

---

3   T and M Batten: The Non-Directive Approach in Group and Community Work; Oxford University Press, 1967.

Children, according to research and the Shema, acquire religion as they do language. This acquisition is rooted in the first few years of life. As children grow, their language, as well as their belief, about God is shaped and corrected by the religious community to which they belong and by direct instruction from their parents, or should be! Additional support about belief in God may be provided by a religious school.

It might be thought that children are already in touch as far as their parents are concerned, but even many church-going parents have given up any overt religious approach to the upbringing of their youngsters, either of a directive or non-directive kind. And this constitutes a major part of the problem concerning how to integrate the young into the worship of the church and to help them continue to grow into it, and not to move away from it when they get older.

Parents need to be reminded of the importance of their role in the overall process of the Christian formation of their children. The Church, in its turn, needs to provide the understanding, guidance and support that so many well-meaning parents require. Of course some parents will feel totally inadequate when it comes to talking about their faith to their off-spring but the 'directive' approach involves more than words; it involves the children being presented with a life-style, an attitude, even postures, which they can find nowhere else,

As a simple example of what I mean, I quote once again from Dr Nelson. When asked what are two things he would tell parents to start doing at home right away to help their children grow spiritually, he first stressed the importance of praying before meals, saying grace. He told this story.

'One day at a meal for Austin Seminary faculty and their families, I saw something that says volumes about how important prayer is for small children. The children were playing in the backyard when it came time to eat. I was sitting at the table with the mother of one of these children. She saved a place for her daughter who didn't want to come in because she was having fun. The adults went ahead with their meal, and after a while the child came in and sat down. She got some food on her plate. She started eating and then stopped. She stopped right away, she bowed her head and reached for her mother's hand. She was quite young, but the point is that the posture, the attitude of prayer, gets instilled early. Obviously this child was in the habit of praying with her mother and her father when they eat their meals.' 4

The cynic in me wants to suggest that one thing that had not been instilled in the youngster was that of obedience, not coming in when summoned, but I will let that pass! But in other respects that child had been influenced by a directive approach in religious formation (note his use of the word 'instilled' – not, perhaps, the best of choices!) but would we dare claim that it had done her any harm?

The second thing that Professor Nelson would tell parents which is another opportunity for a child's growth in the faith to grow exponentially, as it were, is through bed-time prayers together. I can still remember the picture of my mother and father sitting, one on my bed and the other on my brother's, when we were quite small. I can even remember some of the words that were regularly used. But even more I can picture the bowed heads and clasped hands. There was no escape from it, but today I am deeply grateful that there wasn't.

Sometimes in my ministry parents would say to me: 'We don't talk religion with the children. We want them to be free to decide for themselves when they are older and able to make up their own minds.' Some of those parents were a little nonplussed when I pointed out that they had already decided that their children would grow up knowing very little about the Faith, at least from them. Paradoxically, they were being highly directive albeit in a negative kind of way.

All of this calls for a close partnership between the church and the home. The church always needs to be deliberate and helpful in supporting adults in leading a Christian life and encouraging them in their spiritual nurture of their children. When this is conjoined with dedicated teaching in the Junior Church, along with the local congregation providing a warm and welcoming environment for the young, then we can forget about the children's address and other distractions. Let the worship be splendid, something that lifts the heart, speaks home to the depths of our being; something too that brings us back to realities, God at the centre!

---

4   Op.cit, Austin Seminary Journal, Spring 2002, p16.

Children won't be able to articulate this, of course not. But they will be able to sense that there is something wonderful going on, something that they want to grow into rather than that which they want to grow out of.

And we need not be too fussed as to whether they can understand what is taking place. Some of them, anyway, are away ahead of us in that respect!

Chapter Seventeen

'Zeitgeist'

'Zeitgeist'

There is a German word which has now found its way into dictionaries of English and is increasingly beloved by theologians; it is 'Zeitgeist'.

In the Britain of the late 1960s, (*Time* Magazine dubbed them the 'Swinging Sixties', thereby boosting four-fold the UK's number of tourists from the USA), the Italian style in dress was all the rage among the young. It was the immediate successor to the mock-Edwardian style which had given rise to what was called the 'Teddy Boy' (and Girl!) phenomenon. The new fashion consisted of cut-away jackets, a much shorter hair-style in contrast to the flowing locks of the 'Teds' and, above all, 'winkle-picker' shoes. The latter were foot-wear with long pointed toes and derived their name from the phrase 'winkle out', that is to force out gradually by means of a sharp end.

As I was very much involved with the on-going life of the church's youth club, I thought that a bit of incarnational theology in action would not go amiss, and so I decided to be 'with it' and purchased a pair of pointed shoes for myself. Sensibly, as I thought, I did not buy a pair quite so sharp as those worn by the youngsters. I compromised with an in-between pair, but ones which I foolishly judged to be sufficiently in the modern fashion.

I wore them at the next Saturday night dance in the church hall. I sat down to talk with a couple of lads, one leg casually crossed over the other and deliberately swinging a foot gently up and down. After about ten minutes there had been no response and so, nudging Leslie, a youngster who took pride in being in the vanguard of all matters related to the latest mode, I asked:

'What do you think of my new shoes, Les?'
'They're OK, I suppose.'
'What do you mean "I suppose"? Pretty sharp aren't they?'
'Garn! Get lost! They look as if they're still in the box you bought them in'!

As far as Les was concerned, my 'pointed' shoes had no real point at all and I silently had to agree with him. They never appeared again but it still took me some time to learn that there was a difference between being involved with people and being totally identified with them. The notion of total identification carries with it the danger of your own identity, and what values you can bring to a situation, being swallowed up by the surrounding mores; whereas involvement betokens a concern for, and an outreach to, others but one in which your own identity and value-system is not sunk beyond trace.

I shudder when I recall how, as a young minister, I tried many times to be 'with it' but often only succeeded in making a fool of myself. I have, of course, not been alone in this regard. The church at large has often fallen into the same trap only to find that when we get where we think 'It' is, 'It' has moved on apace leaving us with the proverbial egg on our face. In an often quoted remark, Dean Inge, formerly of St Paul's Cathedral, London, said: 'Whoever marries the spirit of this age will find himself a widower in the next.' Today he might have substituted 'Zeitgeist' for 'the spirit of the age', because this is exactly what the translation of this German word means.

There is no doubt that, in recent years, church leaders and members have flirted with the category of 'Zeitgeist', of being 'with it', even falling for that former popular aphorism: 'the world must write the agenda' with its implication that the Church must respond to, and éven follow, secular trends, and not try to lead them, if she is to stay in contention. We have already mentioned those liturgies which go out of their way to be 'user-friendly', and to be entertaining above all else. They are the 'pointed shoes' where modern worship is concerned and are to be viewed with caution. Many of them go the way of all liturgical 'quick fixes.'

In the introduction to this book, it was stated that Reformed worship essentially should reflect the basis of Reformed teaching (theology) which stresses the sovereignty of God, the centrality of God in the life of the individual and in the life of the world: God first. We do not have a monopoly on this over against other Christians, but we have a particular obligation to affirm it boldly by what we say and do in our liturgy. This does not mean we are oblivious to the world, we simply do not take our marching orders from it. For the Christian, sincerity of worship and commitment in service to the world go hand in hand. An incarnational orientated liturgy is *ipso facto* a political liturgy; it will inevitably address the social, political order. But it will do so from the vantage of its transfiguration viewpoint – to use Paul Lehmann's metaphor – and not from a human perspective. This, however, as mentioned in the Introduction, has not been the remit of this book. I have simply taken the importance of this horizontal dimension for granted, while concentrating on the vertical nature of the worship we offer in the sanctuary to the most holy God. A strong emphasis has been made on the importance of form and order in such worship.

At the end of the day, however, all human forms of worship, no matter how well ordered, are, by definition, human forms. This means that whatever we manage to do in church by way of making our worship an acceptable offering in God's sight, we always fall short of the ideal. Bonhoeffer's description, however, of worship in terms of the 'penultimate' is a salutary concept to bear in mind. All our activities in the sanctuary are, even at their best, only by way of rehearsal for that perfect praise which can only be enjoyed in heaven itself. Since a rehearsal is not the final word, there is scope for flexibility, for openness to the unexpected, and even for experiment, provided it is not the world which writes, or directs, the script! But these 'rehearsals' must also learn from the past and from other traditions within the Universal Church. For liturgy must always be seen in an ecumenical context, as today's liturgists are increasingly aware.

The liturgy is ecumenical in four senses. 'First, it is in continuity with and shaped by the liturgical traditions of the Church as they have developed over the centuries. These traditions are rich in their diversity; even the New Testament has different accounts of the Last Supper. But it must not be severed from its roots. Second, in an age of theological and liturgical convergence between separate communions, the liturgy of any one confession needs to be prepared not in isolation from but in dialogue with the liturgies of other churches, so that it is open to enrichment by them. Reformed liturgy is not a new invention; early Reformed liturgies were Reformed masses. It is therefore important to have in mind not only the needs of the moment but also to demonstrate a sense of continuity with the worshipping communities of the Christian ages. Third, the liturgy must enable a respect for legitimate theological pluralism to flourish. It cannot be the expression of a single way of reading or interpreting the Bible and salvation history. Fourth, the world is present in the liturgy in the lives and concerns of the worshippers. The liturgy is a sign of the reconciliation of all things in Christ, of which the life of the Church is the first fruits, never an end in itself.'[1]

In chapter two it was pointed out that today, as opposed to former years, there are many stories clamouring for people's attention, stories by which they seek to make sense of their lives and, as a result, the Christian story is not so prominent or influential as it once was. Even within some parts of the Church there has entered a creeping amnesia where the fullness of the Gospel story is concerned and much present day worship seems to have only a tenuous hold on our foundational faith-narrative. It has been our contention that a better respect for liturgical shape is essential if the Reformed Church is to get its act together and be faithful both to its heritage and to its missionary task.

But shape and order must not have the final word. After all, there are too many examples of worshipping communities in different parts of the world, and in difficult circumstances, who are proclaiming the Gospel of Jesus Christ powerfully, without too much apparent attention to shape and form (though, as we have seen, these are often present though they themselves may not always recognise this!).

Over the last five years I have come into close contact in Africa with worshipping communities which are loosely allied to what is called the Independent Churches Movement. These groups often worship in the open air, partly because they cannot afford buildings large enough to hold them, and partly because they like to be near water for baptismal purposes. By no stretch of the imagination could you say that there was a recognisable form to their services, but nonetheless this interested onlooker could see that the Gospel story was alive and well, and in good hands. Examples from nearer home could be cited to illustrate the same point, examples from the Salvation Army, the Quakers, the Black churches and others. Neither of the first two, for instance, celebrate the sacraments, the importance of which we have been at some pains to highlight, but they could legitimately claim (and often do) that their whole act of worship is sacramental.

---

1   From 'The Draft Order of Service of Holy Communion', offered to the Doctrine, Prayer and Worship Committee of the United Reformed Church, 1998.

Nothing that has been said in the preceding pages should be taken to mean that there is no room for liturgical pluralism in our churches. The aim has been simply to remind those of us within the Reformed tradition, not least those who feel increasingly dissatisfied and 'short-changed' by some of its worship today, that we have here an all-too-often hidden treasure but one which still has the potential to enrich anew, as a 'converting and an edifying ordinance' (John Calvin), which we ignore to our loss.

The true face of the universal Church is indeed revealed in its worship and we have earlier paraphrased the ancient expression, '*lex orandi, lex credendi*', as 'the way you pray determines what you believe.' This praying/worshipping syndrome must not depend on how we happen to be feeling at any given moment, or on what the prevailing Zeitgeist happens to be. The '*lex orandi*' for the Christian is something that has been shaped over many centuries, honed, modified and reformed, and, through it, we are continually called to renewed faith in that which gave rise to it in the first place – the work of God as Creator and Redeemer, that work which came to full focus in the birth, life, death and resurrection of Jesus Christ, and to which, supremely, the Scriptures bear witness.

We must continue in our worship today to be faithful and responsive to that work and, in our particular limb of the Holy, Catholic and Apostolic Church, seek always to follow the Reformation motto: '*ecclesia reformata semper reformanda*,' that is: 'The Church reformed, always in need of being reformed.' We must also seek to ensure that our worship expresses our 'chief and highest end' (pages ix, x) which is to glorify God and fully to enjoy God for ever.

Select Bibliography

A. M. Allchin: *The Dynamic of Tradition*; London: Darton, Longman and Todd,1981.

Horace T. Allen, Jr and Joseph Russell: *On Common Ground*; Norwich: Canterbury Press, 1998.

Horace T. Allen, Jr: *Handbook for the Revised Common Lectionary* (ed. Peter C. Bower); Louisville: Westminster/John Knox.

C. K. Barrett: *Church, Ministry, and Sacraments in the New Testament*; Exeter: The Paternoster Press, 1985.

T & M Batten: *The Non-Directive Approach in Group and Community Work*; Oxford: OUP, 1967.

Richard Baxter: *The Reformed Pastor*; London: SCM Press, 1956.

Peter Berger: *The Sacred Canopy – Elements of a Sociological Theory of Religion*; New York: Doubleday, 1967.

Paul Bradshaw and Bryan Spinks (Eds): *Liturgy in Dialogue*; London: SPCK, 1993.

Peter Brooke: *The Empty Space*; London: MacGibbon & Kee, 1968.

R. E. C. Browne: *The Ministry of the Word*; London: SCM Press, 1958.

Walter Brueggemann: *Finally Comes the Poet*; Minneapolis: Augsburg Fortress Press, 1989.

George B. Burnet: *The Holy Communion in the Reformed Church of Scotland, 1560–1960*; Edinburgh: Oliver and Boyd, 1960.

Ronald P. Byars: *Christian Worship – Glorifying and Enjoying God*; Geneva Press, 2000.

John Calvin: *Institutes of the Christian Religion (two vols)*; Ed. John McNeill, tr. Ford Lewis Battle; London: SCM, 1960.
(Also: 1949 Edition, translated by Henry Beveridge: London: James Clarke & Co).

Henry Sloan Coffin: *The Public Worship of God*; London: The Independent Press,1950.

Patrick Collinson: *The Reformation*; London: Weiden & Nicolson, 2003. (Paperback by Phoenix, 2005).

Oscar Cullmann: *Early Christian Worship*; London: SCM Press, 1953.

Dom Gregory Dix: *The Shape of the Liturgy*; London: Dacre Press, Adam and Charles Black, 1945.

Christopher Elwood: *Calvin for Armchair Theologians*; Louisville/London: Westminster John Knox Press, 2002.

H. H. Farmer: *The Servant of the Word*; London: Nisbett & Co., 1941

John Fenwick and Bryan Spinks: *Worship in Transition – The Twentieth Century Liturgical Movement*; Edinburgh: T & T Clark, 1995.

David Ford: *Theology – A Very Short Introduction*; Oxford: OUP, 1999.

Forrester/McDonald/Tellini: *Encounter with God – An Introduction to Christian Worship and Practice*; Edinburgh: T & T Clark, 1995.

Duncan Forrester and Douglas Murray (Eds): *Studies in the History of Worship in Scotland*; Edinburgh: T & T Clark, 1984.

B. A. Gerrish: *The Old Protestantism and the New – Essays on the Reformation Heritage*; Edinburgh: T & T Clark 1982. [Now in paperback].

B. A. Gerrish: *Grace and Gratitude – The Eucharistic Theology of John Calvin*; Minneapolis: Augsburg Fortress Press, 1993.

Shirley C. Guthrie: *Always Being Reformed – Faith for a Fragmented World*; Louisville: Westminster John Knox Press, 1996.

D. G. Hart: *Recovering Mother Kirk – The Case for Liturgy in the Reformed Tradition*; Grand Rapids: Baker Academic, 2003.

D. G. Hart and John R. Muether: *With Reverence and Awe – Returning to the Basics of Reformed Worship*; Phillipsburg: P & R Publishing Company, 2002.

A. G. Hebert: *Liturgy and Society – The Function of the Church in the Modern World*; London: Faber and Faber, 1935.

Paul Waltman Hoon: *The Integrity of Worship – Ecumenical and Pastoral Studies in Liturgical Theology*; Nashville: Abingdon Press, 1971.

Thomas Hopko: *All the Fulness of God – Essays on Orthodoxy, Ecumenism and Modern Society*; Crestwood, New York: St Vladimir's Seminary Press, 1982.

Michael Ignatieff: *The Russian Album*; London: Vintage Press, 1997.

Robert W. Jenson: *Visible Words – The Interpretation and Practice of Christian Sacraments*; Minneapolis: Fortress Press, 1978.

Leander E. Keck: *The Bible in the Pulpit – The Renewal of Biblical Preaching*; Nashville: Abingdon Press, 1978.

Philip J. Lee: *Against the Protestant Gnostics*; New York: OUP, 1987.

Paul L. Lehmann: *The Decalogue and a Human Future*; Grand Rapids, Michigan: William B. Eerdmans, 1995.

Diarmaid MacCulloch: *Reformation – Europe's House Divided, 1490-1700*; London: Penguin Books, 2004.

John Macquarrie: *A Guide to the Sacraments*; London: SCM, 1997.

Alister E. McGrath: *Reformation Thought – an Introduction*: Oxford: Blackwells, 1993.

T. W. Manson: *The Church's Ministry*; London: Hodder & Stoughton, 1948.

Ernest Marvin: *Odds Against – Young People and the Church*; London: SCM, 1967.

Ernest Marvin (with Micklem, Clark and Gilmore): *Ministry in Question*; London: SCM, 1971.

Ernest Marvin and Ewan Hooper: *A Man Dies*; London: Darton, Longman and Todd, 1964.

William D. Maxwell: *Outline of Christian Worship*; London: OUP, 1946.

William D. Maxwell: *Concerning Worship*; London: Oxford University Press, 1948. Re-issued in 1982 as: History of Christian Worship; Grand Rapids: Baker Book House.

Stephen Mayor: *The Lord's Supper in Early English Dissent*; London: Epworth Press, 1972.

Blair Gilmer Meeks (Ed): *The Landscape of Praise – Readings in Liturgical Renewal*; Pennsylvania: Trinity Press International, 1996.

N. Micklem (Ed): *Christian Worship – Studies in its History and Meaning*; Oxford University Press, 1936.

Richard John Neuhaus: *Freedom for Ministry*; Grand Rapids, Michigan: William B. Eerdmans Publishing Company, 1979.

James Hastings Nichols: *Corporate Worship in the Reformed Tradition*; Philadelphia: Westminster Press, 1990.

Edward Norman: *Entering the Darkness – Christianity and its Modern Substitutes*; London: SPCK, 1991.

Hughes Oliphant Old: *Themes and Variations for a Christian Doxology*; Grand Rapids, Michigan: William B. Eerdmans Publishing Company, 1992.

Hughes Oliphant Old: *Worship that is Reformed According to Scripture*; Atlanta: John Knox Press, 1984.

Douglas F. Ottati: *Reforming Protestantism – Christian Commitment in Today's World*; Louisville: Westminster John Knox Press, 1995.

David Peel: *Reforming Theology*; London: The United Reformed Church, 2002

H. Boone Porter: *The Day of Light – the Biblical and Liturgical Meaning of Sunday*; Greenwich, USA: The Seabury Press, 1966.

Michael Ramsay: *The Christian Priest Today*; London: SPCK, Revised 1985.

Erik Routley: *Christian Hymns Observed*; London: Mowbray, 1983.

James H. Smylie: *A Brief History of the Presbyterians*; Louisville: Geneva Press 1996.

Edward Schillebeeckx: *Ministry – A Case for Change*; London: SCM 1981.

Stephen Sykes: *The Identity of Christianity*; London: SPCK, 1984.

Thomas F. Torrance (Ed): *Theological Dialogue Between Orthodox and Reformed Churches* (chapter 3, Hans-Helmut Essex: The Authority of the Church and Authority in the Church According to the Reformed Tradition): Edinburgh: Scottish Academic Press, 1985.

Tony Tucker: *Reformed Ministry*; London: The United Reformed Church 2003

Evelyn Underhill: *Worship*; London: Nisbet 1948 (fourth reprint of third edition).

Geoffrey Wainwright: *Doxology – The Praise of God in Worship, Doctrine and Life*; London: Epworth, 1980.

Nigel Watson: *Striking Home – Interpreting and Proclaiming the New Testament*; London: Epworth Press, 1987.

Nigel Watson: *First Epistle to the Corinthians*; London: Epworth, 1992.

James F. White: *Introduction to Christian Worship*; Nashville: Abingdon, 1980.

James F. White: *Traditions in Transition*; Louisville: Westminster/John Knox, 1989.

James F. White: *A Brief History of Christian Worship*; Nashville: Abingdon.

Rowan Williams: *Lost Icons – Reflections on Cultural Bereavement*; Edinburgh: T & T Clark, 2000.

Rowan Williams: *Why Study the Past? – The Quest for the Historical Church*; London: Darton, Longman and Todd, 2005.

David Willis and Michael Welker (Eds): *Toward the Future of Reformed Theology*; Grand Rapids, Michigan: William B. Eerdmans, 1999.

H. J. Wotherspoon and J. M. Kirkpatrick: *A Manual of Church Doctrine according to the Church of Scotland*, revised and edited by T. F. Torrance and R. Selby Wright; London: OUP, 1960.

Frances Young: *The Art of Performance*; London: Darton, Longman and Todd, 1990.

Index of persons

Index of subjects